Soup!

Soup!

Hot and cold recipes for all seasons

Pippa Cuthbert &
Lindsay Cameron Wilson

Good Books

Intercourse, PA 17534
800/762-7171
www.goodbks.com

Dedication
To our mothers and grandmothers,
the best soup makers of all

First published in the United States by
Good Books
Intercourse, PA 17534
800/762 - 7171
www.goodbks.com

SOUP!
Good Books, Intercourse, PA 17534
International Standard Book Number: 1-56148-500-4
(paperback edition)
International Standard Book Number: 1-56148-501-2
(comb-bound paperback edition)

Library of Congress Catalog Card Number: 2005014519

Library of Congress Cataloging-in-Publication Data

Cuthbert, Pippa.
    Soup! : hot and cold recipes for all seasons / Pippa
Cuthbert and Lindsay Cameron Wilson.
       p. cm.
Includes bibliographical references and index.
    ISBN 1-56148-500-4 (pbk.) -- ISBN 1-56148-501-2 (plastic comb)
1. Soups. I. Wilson, Lindsay Cameron. II. Title.
    TX757.C88 2005
    641.8'13--dc22
               2005014519

Senior Editor: Clare Hubbard
Editor: Anna Bennett
Design: Paul Wright
Photography: Stuart West
Food styling: Pippa Cuthbert and Lindsay Cameron Wilson
Production: Hazel Kirkman
Editorial Direction: Rosemary Wilkinson

Reproduction by Pica Digital PTE Ltd, Singapore
Printed and bound by Tien Wah Press, Malaysia

Acknowledgments
As always, many thanks to Camilla Schneideman at
Divertimenti (www.divertimenti.co.uk) and Lindy Wiffen at
Ceramica Blue (www.ceramicablue.co.uk) for their gorgeous
props. Thanks also go to friend and tester Cynthia Shupe; to
my mother-in-law Rose Wilson for sharing both culinary
wisdom and her kitchen; to Stuart West for his beautiful
photographs; and to all our friends and family who contributed
in countless ways to this book.

Notes
Due to the slight risk of salmonella, recipes containing raw
eggs should not be served to children, the ill or elderly, or to
pregnant women.

Both imperial and metric measures are given for the recipes –
follow either set of measures, but not a mixture of both as they
are not interchangeable.

Contents

Introduction

Soup: liquid, ingredient, bowl and spoon. It's a simple equation for such a complex concoction. Soups nourish bodies, quench thirsts, titillate appetites and impress palates. They can be velvety smooth, sweetly chilled, hot and spicy or thick and chunky. Every country has a version of its own; every culture has a corresponding etiquette to match. Sipping straight from the bowl is accepted in some countries; in others it is more usual to slurp from a spoon. Some people tip the soup bowl away from them, others tilt it towards them. Certain soups call for chopsticks; others need a knife and fork. Every restaurant has a soup on its menu; every family has a seasonal favorite. Its vast history, countless variations and the myriad books dedicated to the subject are enough to discourage any food writer from putting pen to paper.

Nonsense. Like any good stock, soup recipes must be boiled down, filtered, distilled to perfection. *Soup!* is the result of this process. It's the culmination of our travels, our experiences, our experiments and kitchen sessions. It captures big, global flavors, but employs our signature easy-to-follow techniques. The book is divided into chapters designed to cater to all tastes, from sweet to bitter, salty to sour, *umami* to sparkle. *Umami* and sparkle? Let Pippa and me explain. *Umami* is a Japanese word that has replaced hot as the fifth taste. It is part of a new concept of taste sensations that employs all the senses to identify the savory, pungent, almost meaty flavors found in soy sauce or seaweed-based foods. In 2004, The *New York Times Style Magazine* took the sensation-taste phenomenon one step further by citing "sparkle" as the sixth flavor sensation. Sparkle – the culinary equivalent of bling – describes an effervescent drink or a precious ingredient. Our Special Occasions chapter, even if we say so ourselves, certainly sparkles.

This brings us to stocks, the foundation of all soups. In order for a soup to sparkle in the truest sense of the term, it should be made with a homemade stock. However, life is fast, and stocks can be slow to make. But slow can be easy if you're always thinking one step ahead. Take my aunts, for example. They have trained me in the ways of stock.

1. Aunt Sandra: The family is gathered together at the cottage for the annual lobster feast. It's a warm evening and the sky is aglow – perfect weather. Everyone is sitting outside around a picnic table topped with freshly cooked lobsters and little bowls of warm, melted butter. The mood is jovial, but talk is limited; dining on precious jewels from the sea takes concentration. But as the shells are being cracked and the tender pink meat is carefully excavated from deep within the shells, I notice the concern in my Aunt Sandra's eyes. As the empty shells are carelessly tossed onto the grass below, something very serious is on her mind: what about the shells?

After we feast, she collects the shells and places them back into the lobster pot. To the shells she

adds a bay leaf, some peppercorns, a roughly chopped leek and a few sprigs of thyme from her container garden. She covers the lobster shells with cold water and brings everything to a simmer. In 30 minutes (just enough time to have a glass or two of wine while enjoying the sunset) her stock is ready. She strains it and places it in a freezer container, ready to form the base for impromptu bisques sometime in the future.

2. Aunt Betsy: It's a rainy Sunday evening and Aunt Betsy and Uncle George have just finished a roast chicken dinner. The dishes are stacked but the Red Sox baseball game has just begun. Betsy puts the chicken carcass into a stockpot and adds a few chopped carrots, onions, cloves of garlic and anything else with flavor from the vegetable drawer in the fridge. She covers it all with cold water, sprinkles the lot with a few peppercorns and a few sprigs of fresh herbs, brings it to a boil, and then sets it back to a simmer. Nine innings later she has a pot of chicken stock.

There is no need to be too stringent about using homemade stock, however. If bouillon

granules or cubes are the only option and you would not make soup otherwise, then go with it. But do take the time to find low-salt, even organic varieties, and season sparingly. Commercial stocks are often high in salt and other additives.

So relax in front of the TV and take a sip of wine. Soon your soup will be ready.

To make a soup with depth and substance you must develop the flavor right from the start. Using a flavorsome stock and implementing the right techniques are fundamental in making a delicious soup. Start with a strong foundation and you will always have success when making soup.

The basics of soup

SOFFRITTO

We almost always begin our soups with a preliminary aromatic preparation known as *soffritto* in Italy, literally meaning "to fry gently." This forms the basis of a number of dishes, from soup to risottos and stews to fricassées. For Italians this mixture usually consists of onion, celery, carrot, garlic and bay leaves, but the basic preparation is fundamental in forming underlying flavors in many cuisines around the world. The Spanish predominantly include paprika in their base, while in Latin America tomatoes and peppers form the base flavor. In Southeast Asia shallots, chillies, ginger and garlic dominate, and in North Africa you will find plentiful amounts of cumin and coriander seeds.

We almost always start by sautéing onion or shallots until translucent, then adding garlic and other vegetables as the recipe requires. Avoid adding the onion and garlic at the same time to enable the individual flavors to develop.

A *soffritto* almost always precedes the addition of the main ingredients. The stage that follows, in Italy, is called *insaporire*. This involves stirring the main ingredients, whether meat or vegetables, into the *soffritto* and coating them evenly in the flavor elements of the base before the addition of stock or other liquid.

STOCK

A stock is a liquid to which bones, meat, vegetables, herbs and spices have imparted their flavor. We always encourage the use of fresh, homemade stocks in all our soup recipes, but in this day and age it is unrealistic to expect people to always make their own stock. For this very reason we have included information on some of the many pantry stocks readily available at the supermarket.

Important tips for making homemade stock

• Always use cold water.

• Never boil your stock but instead simmer it for a long time so the fat can rise to the top and be skimmed off. If you boil stock it becomes cloudy and greasy as the fat becomes incorporated.

• Adding a little cold water to the stock while it is simmering will help any impurities or scum to rise to the surface to be skimmed off.

• It is important to skim off the scum that rises to the surface as you go, topping up with extra water if necessary.

• Brown stock is made from cooked bones and white stock from uncooked or cooked bones.

• Aim for evenly sized chunks of vegetable, meat and bone, but they do not have to be perfectly regular, as they will eventually be discarded. However, the smaller the pieces the faster they will flavor the water and the sooner the stock can be used.

• Stock can be reduced for more convenient storage. Reduce the stock by boiling it, uncovered. Stock can be easily reconstituted by the addition of water.

• Stock can be frozen for up to 6 months. Freeze in plastic bags or, if the stock has been reduced, in ice cube trays.

• Stock can be refrigerated for up to 3 days.

• Never season your stock – always save the seasoning for the end result, i.e. the soup you are making.

All stock recipes make approximately 6¼ cups (1.5L)

Chicken stock (white stock)

1 **uncooked chicken carcass or whole chicken about** 2lb 4oz (1kg)
3 **bay leaves**
1 tsp **black peppercorns**
2 **celery sticks,** leaves included, roughly chopped
2 **carrots,** unpeeled, chopped
1 **onion,** unpeeled, halved
3 **sprigs thyme**
9 cups (2L) **cold water**

Put all the ingredients in a large stockpot, adding extra water if necessary to ensure the chicken is covered by about 1in (2.5cm) water. Bring to a gentle simmer and continue to simmer for about 1½–2 hours, skimming off any scum with a large spoon, as the stock simmers. Leave to cool slightly before straining through a fine sieve.

▓ Giblets can also be added to your stock (for the last half hour of cooking), but always use them sparingly as the flavor can be strong and unpleasant.

▓ If you have used a whole chicken you can add the cooked meat to a soup.

Duck stock

1 **duck** (about 4¾lb/2.2kg)
1 **carrot,** unpeeled, sliced
2 **celery sticks,** leaves included, roughly chopped
1 **bay leaf**
3 **sprigs parsley**
3 **sprigs thyme**
8 **black peppercorns**

Put all the stock ingredients in a pan and cover with water. Bring to a boil then simmer for 2½ hours, occasionally skimming off any residue. After 2 hours, remove duck and allow to cool. (Leave remaining stock ingredients to simmer for 30 minutes more.)

Strain remaining stock and cool. If possible, chill stock overnight so fat can solidify on top and be easily removed.

▓ When shredding cooked meat from carcass for use in soup, wear clean rubber gloves. It makes the job easier and much less messy!

Meat stock (brown stock)

2lb 4oz (1kg) **meat bones,**
   preferably veal or beef
1 **onion,** unpeeled, halved
3 **bay leaves**
1 tsp **black peppercorns**
2 **celery sticks,** leaves included,
   roughly chopped
1 **carrot,** unpeeled, chopped
2 **tomatoes,** chopped
2 **sprigs rosemary**
9 cups (2L) **cold water**

Roast the bones in a dry roasting
pan at 400°F/200°C for about 40
minutes. Transfer to a large
stockpot and add the remaining
ingredients. Place the roasting pan,
with a little hot water added, on the
stove and heat, stirring until boiling.
Boil for 2–3 minutes, scraping any
of the sticky residue from the base
and sides of the pan. Add this to
the stockpot. Cover all the
ingredients in the stockpot with
water, adding extra if necessary to
ensure that everything is covered
by about 1in (2.5cm). Bring to a
gentle simmer and simmer for
about 1½–2 hours. Leave to cool
slightly before straining through a
fine sieve.

■ Lamb or pork bones should
be used only when specifically
called for in recipe. Their flavor is
strong and dominating and may
overpower your soup.

Vegetable stock

2 **celery sticks,** leaves included,
   chopped
2 **leeks,** roughly chopped
1 **onion,** unpeeled, halved
2 **carrots,** unpeeled, chopped
1 **head garlic,** cut in half
   horizontally
5 **sprigs parsley**
3 **bay leaves**
5 **sprigs thyme or** 1 **bouquet
   garni**
1 tsp **black peppercorns**
9 cups (2L) **cold water**

Put all the ingredients in a large
stockpot and cover with water,
adding extra if necessary to
ensure everything is covered by
about 1in (2.5cm). Bring to a
gentle simmer, removing any
scum with a large spoon, and
simmer for about 1 hour. Leave to
cool slightly before straining
through a fine sieve.

■ Always use aromatic vegetables
and not starchy vegetables (i.e.
do not use potatoes, pumpkin
etc.) Vegetable peelings and
stalks are also a useful addition to
your vegetable stock.

Fish stock

2lb 4oz (1kg) **cooked or uncooked fish bones or fresh prawns or prawn shells**
1 **onion,** unpeeled, halved
2 **leeks,** chopped
1 **fennel bulb,** quartered
1 tsp **black peppercorns**
3 **sprigs parsley**
2 **celery sticks,** leaves included, chopped
7½ cups (1.75L) **cold water**

Put all the ingredients in a large stockpot and cover with water, adding extra if necessary, to ensure everything is covered by about 1in (2.5cm). Bring to a gentle simmer and simmer for about 20–30 minutes. Strain through a fine sieve immediately.

■ Never simmer your fish stock for a long period of time, as this will result in a bitter flavor.

Oriental stock

4 **shallots,** unpeeled, halved
2 **stalks lemongrass**
3 **kaffir lime leaves**
1 **red chilli,** halved
3 **star anise**
1 **clove garlic**
1-in (2.5-cm) piece **fresh ginger**
1 handful **coriander leaves**
7½ cups (1.75L) **cold water**

Put all the ingredients in a large stockpot and cover with water. Bring to a gentle simmer and simmer for about 20–30 minutes, then strain immediately.

PANTRY STOCKS

Pantry stocks are a cheap and efficient way of enriching soups, stews and gravies. Although generally inferior to fresh stocks, they are still a useful ingredient to have available at all times, especially when you are in a rush. Pantry stocks come in many forms, from bouillon cubes to granules and concentrates to jellies.

Cubes
We bet you all have a stock cube lurking in the cupboard somewhere! Even we have to own up to having an emergency stash. Stock cubes are very widely used and, although not fantastic in flavor, they are a good standby. They can often be very salty, however, so if you are making soup with stock cubes, make sure you do not season your soup until just before serving. One exceptional stock cube that we like to use often is Tom Yum cubes, which are available from many Oriental shops and supermarkets. They impart a hot, chilli-citrus flavor and are extremely useful in Oriental soups and broths.

Granules or powder
These are useful as they dissolve very quickly and can be added directly to boiling water to create a stock. Dashi granules are a particular favorite of ours and are useful in Japanese cooking and miso soups.

Concentrates
These can also be added directly to boiling water. Only a small amount is usually needed as the flavor is more concentrated and reduced. Buy a bottle and it will last a long time.

Jellies
Jellies are particularly useful for making glazes and brushing over meats. You will always pay more for jellies than cubes and granules, but the flavor is often superior.

Equipment

Blender
A blender is probably the most essential piece of equipment in any soup kitchen and it will make very light work of blending soups. A proper, standing blender (not an attachment for the food processor) can usually blend up to 7½ cups (1.75L) of liquid at one time. The end result is achieved easily and speedily and the finished product is always smooth and uniform in texture.

Hand-held blender
Hand-held blenders require a little more work than standing blenders. It is up to you to work them into every corner and purée every lump of vegetable. The end result is usually not as smooth and uniform as that achieved with a standing blender, but the advantage is that cleaning is quick and easy. Hand-held blenders make little mess and can even be used directly in the saucepan the soup has been cooked in. What you use is a matter of personal preference.

Food processor
You can use a food processor instead of a blender to purée your soup, but we always find that this makes more mess than necessary. The soup tends to spill over and you never quite achieve the uniform smoothness that you get with a blender. These days most food processors come with an additional blender attachment, but the volume they hold never seems to be as much as with a standing blender. If money and space are limited, however, then a food processor will do the job adequately – just be at the ready to clean up the mess and be prepared to purée your soup in smaller batches.

Mouli-légumes

A mouli-légumes, or vegetable mill, purées in the same way as a blender or food processor, but also strains fibrous materials that a blender would incorporate into the soup. It is particularly useful for removing tomato skins and fibrous celery strings from your soup. Mouli-légumes usually come with two different-sized metal milling discs. Choose your disc depending on the desired pulpiness of the end product.

Sieve

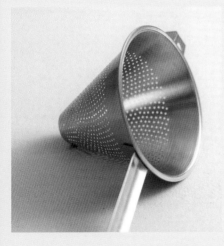

You will need a fine-gauge mesh sieve for puréeing soups, and this is the second best option after a mouli-légumes. Always buy a stainless steel sieve to avoid rusting. A wooden spoon is the best tool to push the soup through the sieve.

Mandoline

A mandoline cutter is an incredibly sharp and potentially dangerous tool in the wrong hands. It enables you to cut uniformly sized slices and julienne strips with ease. It is not necessary to cut perfectly julienned vegetables for a soup that is going to be blended, but for many Oriental soups (where appearance is important) and for garnishing, a mandoline can be very useful – just use it with care.

Stockpot

After the blender, this is the most important piece of equipment to have if you are going to make a lot of soup. Ideally a pot with a 6-quart (6-L) capacity will be adequate for any domestic soup production and certainly for any of our recipes.

Peeler

The swivel peeler (upright or Y–shaped) has been a revelation and you can easily buy one for very little money. It peels thinly and quickly with very little effort.

Colander

A colander is the safest way to strain a stockpot of boiling liquids. Always buy a free-standing colander for extra stability, and the larger it is the better.

Scales
Even in this day and age it is necessary to have scales with both imperial and metric measures. The most technically advanced and efficient are electronic scales, usually battery-operated, that enable you to jump from metric to Imperial at the press of a button. The main advantage is that these scales can be reset to zero as each ingredient is added. Balance scales require two sets of weights (one for metric and one for imperial). They can be attractive, but take up a lot more space in your kitchen. Spring scales show the weight on a calibrated "clock-like" face. Bear in mind that scales vary in their maximum weighing capacity, so make sure you buy scales that suit your particular requirements.

Ladle
A ladle, another "must-have" piece of equipment for making and serving soup, is essential for transferring hot soup from the pot to the bowl without mess and splashing.

Tureen
To serve your soup in true French style you may want to invest in a soup tureen – a large, deep serving dish with a lid for serving soups and stews at the table.

Handy hints

To roast peppers...

Wash red, yellow, orange or green peppers and place them in a preheated 425°F/220°C oven until they start to blister and brown, turning once during cooking. This takes about 25 minutes. Remove from the oven and set aside until cool enough to handle. Peel off the skin and remove the seeds, stalk and membrane from the peppers. Roasted peppers can be frozen or refrigerated for up to 1 week in a plastic bag or covered container.

To skin tomatoes...

Using a small, sharp knife, make a criss-cross slit in the skin at each end of the tomato. Put the tomatoes in a heatproof bowl large enough to cover them with water. (I put the bowl in the sink at this point, under the tap.) Pour boiling water over the tomatoes to cover. Leave until all the little bubbles, coming from the tomatoes, start to subside – about 1–2 minutes. Run cold tap water over the bowl of tomatoes until they are cool. Remove from the water and peel the skin from the flesh. Cut into quarters, removing the seeds and the core also if called for in the recipe you are making.

To cook dried beans...

Rinse the dried beans under cold running water and put in a large bowl. Add enough water to cover the beans by at least 3in (7.5cm) and leave to soak for about 12 hours or overnight. Drain and rinse the beans and put them, together with 3 bay leaves (if you have any), in a saucepan large enough to cover them with at least 3in (7.5cm) water. Do not salt the water – this will make them toughen. Cover the saucepan and bring the water to a boil. Reduce the heat, uncover and simmer for about 45 minutes to 1 hour, or until the beans are tender but not mushy. Keep the beans in the cooking liquid until you are ready to use them so they don't dry out.

To caramelize onions...
Peel four onions and cut them in half. Slice the onions into thin rings and set aside. Heat 4 Tbsp olive oil in a large heavy-based frying pan or sauté pan. Add the onions and stir until evenly coated in the oil. Add 2 tsp extra-fine sugar, stir to combine, then reduce the heat. Leave the onions to caramelize gently over the heat, stirring occasionally until

golden and sticky. This takes about 20–30 minutes.

To roast garlic...
Cut the required number of garlic heads in half horizontally and rub with an even coating of oil (you will need about 2 tsp per garlic head). Put in an oven dish or on a baking pan and roast in a preheated oven at 325°F/170°C for about 40–45 minutes, or until soft to the touch and squeezable. Roasted garlic can be stored, covered, in the fridge for up to 3 days and is delicious added to soups and risottos instead of raw garlic. It is also great spread on bruschetta and crostini as an accompaniment to soup.

To poach a chicken...
First remove the giblets from the cavity and rinse the chicken under cold running water. Place in a large saucepan or stockpot and cover with cold water to 2in (5cm) above the top of the chicken. Bring to a gentle simmer, cover and cook for about 40 minutes, or until cooked through (this is for a 2lb 12-oz (1.25-kg) chicken – adjust times accordingly). Turn off the heat and rest the chicken for 5 minutes in the water before removing, cooling and shredding.

To poach chicken breasts or fish fillets...

Put the chicken breasts or fish fillets in a sauté pan or frying pan and cover with water, stock or milk. Bring to a boil, reduce the heat and simmer, uncovered, until cooked. The fish should turn white and flake easily under a fork, which takes about 5 minutes. Chicken takes longer to cook right through and usually takes about 10–12 minutes for a standard sized breast. When cooked, remove the fish or chicken with a slotted spoon.

To make a white sauce...

Heat 9fl oz (250ml) milk in a heavy-based saucepan and bring to near-boiling point. Melt 1 Tbsp butter in a saucepan, then add 1 Tbsp plain flour and cook for about 30 seconds to 1 minute until foaming. (This is called a roux.) Remove from heat and slowly whisk in the hot milk. Return to the heat and bring to a boil, whisking constantly until thick. Season with salt and pepper and simmer for about 15 minutes. To make a béchamel sauce add 1 halved onion, 3 bay leaves and 1 tsp peppercorns to the milk while heating, and strain before adding to the roux. Season with a little finely grated nutmeg at the end.

To crush garlic...

Chop the garlic roughly on a board and sprinkle a pinch of salt over it. Using the flat edge of a large cook's knife, crush the garlic. The salt helps amalgamate the juices and breaks down the garlic, giving you a paste.

To roast red beets...

Preheat the oven to 400°F/200°C. Remove stalks and leaves from beets. Place in a roasting pan, add about 1 Tbsp oil and toss to coat. Roast, depending on size, for about 30–40 minutes, or until tender.

To make herb-infused oils...

Process 4½ cups (100g) of your chosen herb (such as basil or coriander) with ½ cup (100ml) extra virgin olive oil. Blend for 1–2 minutes to make a paste. Line a bowl with muslin and scrape the paste into it. Gather up the sides of the muslin and squeeze, pushing through as much of the herb-infused oil as possible. Can be stored in an airtight container for up to 2 weeks.

In recipes, fruits/vegetables/ herbs should be washed well before use and prepared in the usual way i.e. trimmed/ peeled/deseeded etc., unless otherwise stated.

Classic

Classic soups, if compared to classical architecture, should conform to an established standard or principle. They should be perfectly symmetrical, with an evenly balanced ratio of flavors. Their style should be refined yet restrained.

This chapter includes those soups in our repertoire that we believe have lasting significance. They are based on the closest that we, as home cooks, could come to the established standard of classic soup-making principles. Classical rules aside, what would a soup cookbook be without a handful of well-established favorites?

Favorite soup recipes, of course, vary from person to person, so what is classic to us could be totally foreign to you. This collection, therefore, covers all obvious bases. Yet beneath the generic titles are rich flavors, exciting twists and original interpretations.

And like any good Corinthian column, perhaps these soups will endure through the ages.

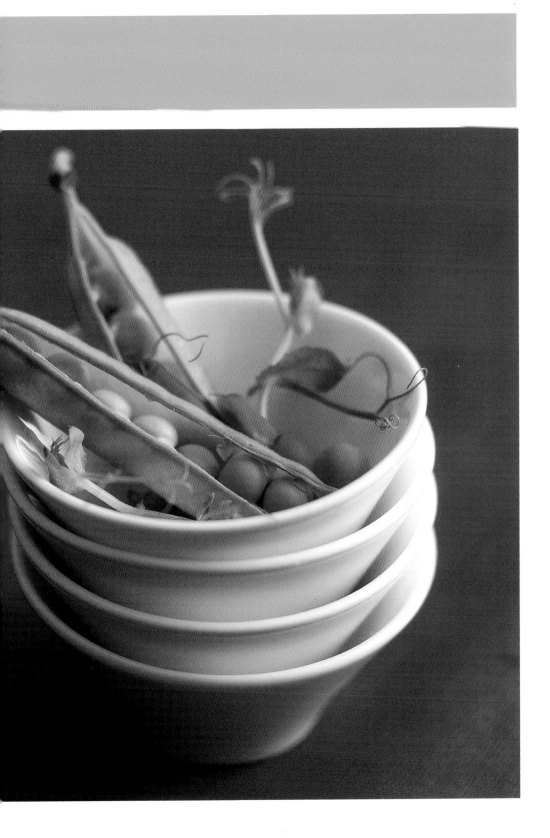

Carrot and ginger soup

Revitalizing

This recipe is based on the classic carrot and ginger soup at Chives Canadian Bistro in my hometown of Halifax. Sadly, they don't share recipes but after many questions and lots of testing, I think this version is not far off.

Serves 4

1 Tbsp **butter**
1 Tbsp **olive oil**
1 **onion,** chopped
2 **cloves garlic,** crushed
1 Tbsp **very finely chopped fresh ginger**
2 tsp **ground cumin**
1 tsp **curry powder**
1lb 10oz (750g) **carrots,** chopped
1 **large potato,** diced
1 **sweet potato,** diced
6¼ cups (1.5L) **chicken stock (see page 12)**
1 Tbsp **runny honey**
½ tsp **salt**
¼ tsp **pepper**

Melt the butter and oil in a large pan over medium heat. Add the onion, garlic and ginger and sauté over low heat until golden, about 10 minutes. Add the cumin and curry powder and continue to sauté for a further minute. Add the vegetables and stock and simmer until the vegetables are tender, about 30 minutes.

Purée in batches until smooth and sieve back into the pot over low heat. Stir in the honey, salt and pepper. If liked, garnish with a mix of shredded mint (1 Tbsp), grated carrot (1 Tbsp), toasted sesame seeds (1 tsp) and honey (2 Tbsp).

Carrot and ginger soup

Asparagus soup

Vivid

A vibrant, velvety soup that's perfect in springtime when asparagus is in season.

Serves 4

1 Tbsp **butter**
1 Tbsp **olive oil**
1 **large leek,** finely chopped
4 Tbsp **finely chopped shallots**
2lb 4oz (1kg) **asparagus,** chopped into ¾-in (2-cm) pieces
½ tsp **salt**
¼ tsp **pepper**
¼ tsp **cayenne**
2¼ cups (500ml) **chicken stock (see page 12)**
2 Tbsp (75ml) **heavy cream**

Optional to serve:
8 additional **asparagus stems,** for dipping
1 tsp **olive oil**
Sea salt and black pepper
4 **eggs**

Melt the butter with the olive oil in a large saucepan over medium heat. Add the leeks and shallots and sauté until the leeks are tender, about 10 minutes. Stir in the asparagus, salt, pepper, cayenne and stock and simmer, stirring occasionally until the asparagus is just tender, about 10 minutes. Purée the soup in batches, then strain through a sieve. Return to the pan; add the cream and heat gently. Taste for seasoning, and serve.

To serve: preheat the oven to 400°F/200°C. Toss the asparagus in oil, place on a baking pan and roast for 6 minutes, or until just tender. Season with sea salt and black pepper. Set aside. While the asparagus is roasting and the soup is gently heating after being puréed, place the eggs in a saucepan of cold water. Bring to a boil and boil gently for 2½ minutes, then rinse quickly under cold water and shell. Serve the soup immediately with the eggs and roasted asparagus on the side.

Leek and potato soup

Comforting

The classic chilled leek and potato soup, known as Vichyssoise, was created in the early twentieth century by a French chef, Louis Diat. Here is our version of this famous soup, with the optional addition of a few caraway seeds. Equally delicious served hot or chilled.

Serves 4

2 tsp **olive oil**
¼ stick (25g) **butter**
½ tsp **caraway seeds** (optional)
1lb 2oz (500g) **leeks,** about 4–5 medium
1 **onion,** finely chopped
1lb 5oz (600g) **potatoes,** cut into ¾-in (2-cm) cubes
3½ cups (800ml) **chicken or vegetable stock (see pages 12–13)**
1¼ cups (300ml) **heavy cream**
Salt and freshly ground black pepper to taste
2 Tbsp **chopped chives**

Heat the olive oil and butter in a large saucepan. Add the caraway seeds, if using, with the leek and onion and sweat until translucent and soft. Add the potato and stock and bring to a boil. Reduce the heat and simmer for 15–20 minutes, or until the potato is cooked.

Remove from the heat and purée in a food processor or blender until smooth. Return to the saucepan, add the cream and bring back to a boil. Season to taste and serve sprinkled with chives.

■ If you would prefer a less creamy soup, try substituting milk for the cream or increase the amount of stock used and add the cream to serve – delicious either way.

Beef and vegetable soup

Warming

When my mother got married she was sent away with this recipe in her suitcase. Her mother and her mother's mother have been making it for as long as anyone can remember. It's a particular favorite in our home, especially on cold, Canadian winter days.

Serves 4–6

1lb (500g) **beef shanks**
9 cups (2L) **cold water**
1 **onion,** finely chopped
3 **celery sticks,** finely chopped
3 **carrots,** finely chopped
2 **parsnips,** finely chopped
1 **turnip,** finely chopped
2 **potatoes,** finely chopped
1–2 tsp **salt,** according to taste
½ tsp **freshly ground black pepper**
1 **bay leaf**

Place shanks in a large pot and cover with the cold water. Simmer for 2 hours. Add remaining ingredients and continue to simmer, stirring occasionally until vegetables are tender, about 45 minutes. Remove shanks with a slotted spoon and cut off any remaining meat. Return meat to the pot and discard bone. Serve with more salt and pepper to taste.

▉ *Finely chopping the vegetables allows the richness of the beef stock to penetrate through the soup.*

Italian meatball and vegetable soup

Savory

This soup can be made using any ground meat you like, such as lamb or chicken. Here, I have used beef

Serves 4

For meatballs
1lb 2oz (500g) **lean ground beef**
½ cup (50g) **fresh bread crumbs**
1 **egg**, beaten
2 Tbsp **chopped fresh oregano or parsley**
Salt and black pepper

1 Tbsp **olive oil**
1 **onion**, finely chopped
1–2 **large red chillies**, finely diced
1 **clove garlic**, crushed
2 **carrots**, diced
1 **zucchini**, diced
3½oz (100g) **cavalo nero**
1 Tbsp **tomato paste**
14-oz (400-g) **can chopped tomatoes**
4½ cups (1L) **beef stock** (see page 13)
Salt and black pepper
2 Tbsp **chopped fresh oregano or parsley**
Parmesan cheese to serve

Put the meatball ingredients in a food processor. Season. Blitz until the mixture comes together in a ball. Set aside.

Heat the olive oil in a large saucepan. Add the onion and chilli and sauté until softened but not browned. Add the garlic, carrots, zucchini, cavalo nero and tomato paste and cook for a further 2–3 minutes or until the vegetables turn a bright color. Add the tomatoes and stock and bring to a boil. Reduce the heat to a slow simmer.

Shape the meatball mixture into teaspoon-sized balls. Drop into the pan one by one, stirring every now and again. Increase the heat slightly and simmer the soup for a further 15–20 minutes or until the meatballs are cooked through. Season. Add the herbs and serve with grated cheese.

Chicken soup with tarragon

Rejuvenating

Chicken soup or broth is often served as a restorative meal to the sick. This soup is slightly more substantial than a broth but will still help soothe any lingering ailments you may have.

Serves 4–6

2lb 4oz (1kg) **chicken,** giblets removed and chicken rinsed
2 **bay leaves**
1 Tbsp **black peppercorns**
1 **small bunch thyme**
2 **onions,** 1 chopped and 1 finely diced
4 **celery sticks,** 2 chopped and 2 finely diced
4 **carrots,** 2 chopped and 2 finely diced
12 cups (3L) **water**
½ stick (50g) **butter**
Salt and black pepper
⅓ cup (40g) **flour**
1 cup (20g) **fresh tarragon**

Put the chicken in a large stockpot. Add the bay leaves, peppercorns, thyme, and the chopped onion, celery and carrots. Add the water and bring to a boil over moderate heat. Reduce the heat and simmer for about 40 minutes or until the chicken is cooked. Remove the chicken from the stock. Set aside. Strain the stock and set aside, discarding the vegetables.

Heat the butter in the same stockpot. Add the finely diced onion, celery and carrots and sauté until the onion is translucent and the vegetables brightly colored. Season. Add the flour and stir constantly until the roux cooks slightly. Add a small amount of the stock and stir. Slowly add a further 6¼ cups (1.5L) of the stock and bring to a simmer.

While the soup is simmering, shred the chicken flesh from the carcass using a fork – be careful, as it will still be hot. Add the shredded chicken and the tarragon to the broth, bring back to a boil and season to taste.

Chicken soup with tarragon

French onion soup

French onion soup

Rich

A soup that needs no introduction. Use a good-quality, rich beef stock for this. The croûtons can be made in advance.

Serves 4

2 Tbsp **olive oil**
¼ stick (30g) **butter**
1lb 14oz (850g) (about 4) **onions, thinly sliced**
2 **cloves garlic, crushed**
1 tsp **granulated sugar**
5 cups (1.2L) **beef stock** (see page 13)
generous 1 cup (250ml) **dry white wine**
Salt and freshly ground black pepper
2 Tbsp **cognac (optional)**
8–12 **Croûtons** (see page 156)
scant 2 cups (200g) **grated Gruyère cheese**
Chopped parsley (optional)

Heat the oil and butter together in a large saucepan until very hot. Add the onions, garlic and sugar and stir for about 5 minutes until they start to darken on the edges. Reduce the heat to very low and leave to cook for a further 20–25 minutes, stirring very occasionally. The onions should caramelize and the base of the pan should have a dark caramelized film on it.

Add the stock and wine. Bring to a boil, scraping the film off the base of the pan. Reduce heat and simmer, uncovered, for about 50 minutes. Season to taste.

Bring the soup back to boiling point before serving and add the cognac if desired. Ladle the soup into heatproof bowls, top with croûtons and sprinkle with the Gruyére cheese. Place the bowls under the grill until the cheese is bubbling and golden. Sprinkle with chopped parsley if liked and serve immediately.

Chicken noodle soup
Cleansing

Quick, simple and rejuvenating, this soup is always a hit!

Serves 4–6

1 **whole small chicken,** about 2lb 4oz (1kg),
   giblets removed and chicken rinsed
3 **bay leaves**
1 Tbsp **black peppercorns**
2 **cloves garlic**
12 cups (3L) **water**
2 **carrots,** finely diced
2 **celery sticks,** finely diced
3½oz (100g) **filini pasta shapes**
1 tsp **salt,** or to taste
Freshly ground black pepper

Put the chicken in a large stockpot. Add the bay leaves, peppercorns and garlic and cover with the water. Bring gently to a boil, over a moderate heat. Reduce the heat and simmer for about 40 minutes or until the chicken is cooked.

Remove the chicken from the stock and set aside. Strain the stock through a sieve and set aside, discarding the bay leaves, peppercorns and garlic. Rinse the stockpot and return 6¼ cups (1.5L) of stock to the pan. Return to the heat, add the carrots, celery and pasta, and bring to a boil. While the stock is coming back to a boil, shred the meat from the chicken and add to the pan. Reduce the heat and simmer for about 10 minutes or until the pasta is cooked and the carrots are tender. Season to taste and serve immediately. If you are not serving immediately, the pasta will keep absorbing the stock. Keep the remaining stock from the chicken and add more just before serving.

Chicken chilli soup

Robust

Thanks to Jeanette O'Reilly, a family friend and wonderful cook from Mississippi, for sharing this recipe with us. Jeanette serves it with hot, cornbread muffins. Delish.

Serves 6–8

1 Tbsp **vegetable oil**
2 **onions,** chopped
2 **cloves garlic,** crushed
6 **chicken breasts,** cut into bite-size pieces
4½ cups (1L) **chicken stock (see page 12)**
2 x 14-oz (400-g) cans **cannelini beans,** rinsed and drained
2 x 14-oz (400-g) cans **cannelini beans,** rinsed, drained
    and mashed with fork
2 x 8-oz (200-g) cans **green chillies,** drained and finely chopped
1 tsp **salt**
1 tsp **dried oregano**
1 tsp **ground cumin**
½ tsp **chilli powder**
½ tsp **black pepper**
⅛ tsp **ground cloves**
⅛ tsp **ground red pepper**

To garnish
generous 1 cup (250ml) **sour cream**
Parsley or coriander

Heat the oil in a large pan over medium heat. Add onions and sauté until they begin to soften, about 5 minutes. Add garlic and chicken and sauté over medium-high heat for about 10 minutes, stirring often. Stir in stock and remaining ingredients. Bring to a boil, cover and simmer for 30 minutes. Garnish with sour cream and parsley or coriander.

Mixed mushroom soup

Autumnal

Madeira adds a luxurious depth to this autumnal, classic soup. This is best made a day ahead.

Serves 4–6

¼ cup (20g) **mixed dried wild mushrooms (shiitake, morels or porcini)**
1 Tbsp **butter**
1 Tbsp **olive oil**
2 **onions**, chopped
6¾ cups (500g) **button mushrooms**, chopped
½ cup (125ml) **Madeira or sherry**
4½ cups (1L) **chicken stock** (see page 12)
½ tsp **salt**
¼ tsp **pepper**
Chopped parsley, to garnish

Soak the dried mushrooms in 1 generous cup (250ml) boiling water for ½ hour. Strain, reserving the soaking liquid. Chop the mushrooms into small pieces and then set aside.

Melt the butter with the olive oil in a large saucepan over medium heat. Add the onion and sauté until golden, about 10 minutes. Add the button mushrooms and sauté until their juices are released. Add the wild mushrooms, the reserved soaking liquid and the Madeira. Stir for 30 seconds, then add the stock and salt and pepper. Partially cover and simmer for 15 minutes. Serve and garnish.

▓ *Madeira is a fortified wine from the Portuguese-owned island of the same name.*

▓ *This soup can be blended before serving, but hand-chopped mushrooms add a rustic quality.*

Mixed mushroom soup

Pea and ham soup

Pea and ham soup

Warming

I remember large pots of this soup bubbling on the stove when I was a child. Mom used to, and still does, make the best pea and ham soup ever! She never followed a recipe so this is my interpretation – I hope it's up to her standard.

Serves 4

3 Tbsp **olive oil**
1 **large onion,** finely chopped
2 **carrots,** finely diced
1 **celery stick,** finely diced
Freshly ground black pepper
3 **bay leaves**
1 **ham hock**
1¾ cups (400g) **yellow or green dried split peas,** rinsed
Water to cover
2½ cups (300g) finely sliced **cabbage**
Salt

Heat the oil in a large stockpot. Add the onion, carrot and celery and sauté for about 10 minutes or until soft but not browned. Season generously with black pepper, then add the bay leaves. Add the ham hock and split peas and stir to combine. Cover generously with cold water and bring to a boil. Reduce the heat and simmer, uncovered, for 1½–2 hours or until the meat is falling off the bone.

Remove the bay leaves and ham hock from the pan and remove any extra meat from the bone. Discard the bone and add the meat to the pan with the sliced cabbage. Bring back to a boil, season with salt and black pepper, then serve.

Bacon, ham and vegetable soup

Aromatic

I'm convinced my husband's NFL football team won the Super Bowl this year because we were watching while eating this soup. Not only is it an intensely flavorful soup, but good things happen when you eat it.

Serves 8

5 slices **smoked bacon**
2 **large leeks**, white part only, finely sliced
4 **celery sticks**, chopped
4 **fat garlic cloves**, crushed
2 Tbsp **chopped fresh rosemary**
2 **large carrots**, chopped
3 **parsnips**, chopped
9 cups (2L) **vegetable stock (see page 13)**
Ham bone
14oz (400g) **cooked, diced ham**
½ tsp **black pepper**
Large handful **flat leaf parsley**, chopped

Heat a large heavy pan over medium heat. Add bacon and cook until crisp. Remove bacon with a slotted spoon, crumble and set aside. Add leeks and celery to bacon drippings and sauté over medium heat, stirring occasionally until soft, about 10 minutes. Add garlic and rosemary and cook for 1 minute. Add carrots, parsnips, stock, ham bone, diced ham and pepper and bring to a boil. Reduce heat and simmer, uncovered, for 30-40 minutes until vegetables are tender. Serve topped with parsley and crumbled bacon.

■ *I like to make this soup with leftover roast ham that's been baked in a maple glaze – it adds a delicious sweetness.*

Ham, potato and chive chowder

Creamy

This soup is a real favorite among children. Ham and potato in a velvety, cheesy broth make for the perfect Sunday lunchtime warmer.

Serves 4

¾ stick (100g) **unsalted butter**
1 **onion,** finely chopped
1lb 5oz (600g) **red potatoes,** chopped into ½-in
   (1-cm) cubes
3 Tbsp **flour**
4½ cups (1L) **vegetable stock (see page 13)**
1 cup (100g) **grated mature cheddar cheese**
10oz (300g) **cooked ham,** cut into ½-in (1-cm) cubes
2 Tbsp **chopped chives**
Salt and freshly ground black pepper, to taste

Melt the butter in a stockpot or heavy-based saucepan. Add the onion and sauté for 2–3 minutes or until translucent but not browned. Add the potato and stir to coat in oil. Add the flour and stir continuously for 1 minute before slowly adding the stock. Bring to a boil and reduce the heat. Add the grated cheddar cheese and stir until melted. Allow the soup to simmer for a further 8–10 minutes. Add the ham and chives and cook for a further 2–3 minutes. Season to taste and serve.

■ *Variation: if you prefer, you can use bacon or pancetta instead of ham. Add the bacon or pancetta with the onion and sauté until cooked before adding the potato.*

Pea and mint soup

Fresh

Fresh baby green peas shelled from the pod and put straight into the pot would be heavenly but a hugely labor-intensive task. This soup is quick and easy to make with the use of frozen petits pois (petite peas). They give the sweetness and color that we desire without hours of slaving in the kitchen.

Serves 4

3½ cups (1kg) **frozen petits pois (petite peas)**
4½ cups (1L) **chicken stock (see page 12)**
½ cup (10g) **fresh mint leaves,** plus extra to garnish
½ cup (100ml) **heavy cream,** plus extra to garnish
Salt and freshly ground black pepper

Put the peas and stock in a medium saucepan and bring to a boil. Turn off the heat, add the mint leaves, and let stand for 5 minutes. Transfer to a blender and liquidize until smooth. You may need to do this in two batches. If you prefer an extra-smooth soup, then pass through a fine sieve. I like to leave the texture and speckled appearance but it's up to you. Return the soup to the pan and add the cream. Taste and season as required. Bring back to a boil before serving. Garnish with extra cream and mint leaves.

■ *This soup is delicious served hot or cold and I like to serve it with poppy seed-topped Grissini (see page 154) or chunky bread on the side.*

■ *If you have made the soup using fresh peas, you may have a pea shoot that you can use as a garnish, as we have.*

Pea and mint soup

Roasted pumpkin soup

Autumnal sweetness

Roasting the vegetables with butter and maple syrup elevates the classic pumpkin soup to sparkling, Cinderella status.

Serves 4–6

1 small pumpkin, about 4lb 8oz (2kg)
1 butternut squash, about 4lb 8oz (2kg)
4 Tbsp butter
4 Tbsp maple syrup or brown sugar
1 large carrot, roughly chopped
1 large red onion, cut into eight pieces
5 cups (1.2L) chicken or vegetable stock (see pages 12–13)
1 head garlic
1 Tbsp Dijon mustard
1 tsp salt
½ tsp pepper

Preheat the oven to 350°F/180°C. Cut the pumpkin and squash into quarters. Scoop out the seeds and discard. Arrange the quarters, skin-side down, in a roasting pan (use two if necessary). Place ½ Tbsp butter and ½ Tbsp maple syrup into the cavity of each pumpkin and squash quarter. Arrange the carrot and onion around the pumpkin and squash. Pour 2¼ cups (500ml) of the stock around the vegetables and cover the pan tightly with foil. Wrap the garlic head in foil. Place the roasting pan and wrapped garlic on oven racks. Roast for 2 hours.

Allow the vegetables to cool slightly. Scoop the flesh from the pumpkin and squash and place in a large saucepan. Discard the skin. Add the onion, carrot and any juice. Unwrap the garlic head and squeeze the roasted pulp from the skins into the pot. Add the mustard, salt, pepper and remaining stock. Bring to a boil, then simmer for 10 minutes. Purée the soup in batches and return to pot. Reheat gently and serve.

Vegetable soup

Ambrosial

The secret to this soup's robust flavor is the addition of Parmesan rind during the long, gentle simmer.

Serves 4

8 Tbsp **olive oil**
½ stick (50g) **butter**
3 **onions,** finely sliced
4 **large carrots,** finely diced
2 **celery sticks,** finely diced
1 **sweet potato,** finely diced
1½ cups (150g) **green beans,** sliced into 1¼-in (3-cm) lengths
2 cups (450g) finely diced **zucchini**
1 bunch **cavelo nero or** ½ head **savoy cabbage,** thinly sliced
14-oz (400-g) can **cherry or plum tomatoes**
2 Tbsp **tomato purée**
4½ cups (1.5L) **chicken or vegetable stock (see pages 12–13)**
Parmesan rind (see tip below)
½ tsp **salt**
Freshly ground black pepper to taste

Heat the oil and butter in a large stockpot over medium heat. Add the onions and reduce the heat to medium-low. Sweat until soft, about 5 minutes. Add the carrots, celery and sweet potato. Sauté for a further 5 minutes. Add the beans and cook for 2–3 minutes, then add the zucchini and cabbage and sauté for a further 5 minutes. Stir in the tomatoes and their juice, the tomato purée, stock, Parmesan rind and salt. Cover and gently simmer for 2½ hours, stirring occasionally. Remove rind and stir in pepper.

▓ *Look for* Parmigiano Reggiano *with the rind still attached. Once the cheese is grated, wrap the rind in plastic wrap and chill. Or, if using immediately, roughly grate the exterior to remove any excess wax and add the rind to the soup.*

Tomato soup

Tomato soup
Pulpy

During my student apartment-sharing days, my roommate Sophie Hartnell's mother, Kate, used to make this for us on a regular basis. All the credit for this recipe must go to her.

Serves 4

2 Tbsp **olive oil**
2 **large onions**, finely chopped
10 **cloves garlic**, roughly chopped
4lb 8oz (2kg) **tomatoes**, cut into quarters
4 **celery sticks**, leaves included, cut into 1-in (2.5-cm) pieces
6 **whole cloves**
6 **sprigs parsley**
1 **large bunch basil**, about 1 cup (20g)
½–1 tsp **white pepper**
scant ¼ cup (30g) **extra-fine sugar** or to taste
Sea salt and freshly ground black pepper to taste

To garnish:
Sprigs of parsley

Heat the oil in a large saucepan. Add the onions and garlic and cook until they begin to sweat, but do not allow them to brown. Add the tomatoes, celery, cloves, parsley, basil, white pepper and sugar. Bring to the boil, reduce the heat and simmer until reduced to a pulp, about 40 minutes.

Pass the pulp through a mouli-légumes or fine sieve. Return the tomato mixture to the pan and bring back to a boil. Taste and add additional sugar, salt and pepper if necessary. If the soup is too concentrated for your liking, dilute it by adding water to taste. Garnish.

Bacon, leek, potato and gruyère soup

Wintry

A creamy, chowder-like soup crowned with crisp baguette slices and bubbling cheese – what could be better?

Serves 4–6

5 slices **back bacon**
1 **large leek,** white part only, chopped
1 **onion,** chopped
2 **large red potatoes,** chopped
3 Tbsp **flour**
2 Tbsp **grainy mustard**
1 tsp **salt**
½ tsp **black pepper**
generous 3 cups (750ml) **milk**
generous 1 cup (250ml) **chicken stock (see page 12)**
3½ cups (400g) grated **Gruyère cheese**
1 tsp **Worcestershire sauce**
8 slices **of day-old baguette**
Small bunch of **parsley,** chopped

Heat a large, ovenproof pot over medium-high heat. Add bacon and cook until crisp. Remove with a slotted spoon, crumble and set aside. Add leek and onion to bacon dripping and sauté until soft, about 7 minutes. Add potatoes and cook for 1 minute more. Stir in flour, mustard, salt and pepper and cook for 3 minutes.

Add milk and stock and gently simmer for 20 minutes or until potatoes are cooked through. Add 2½ cups (300g) of Gruyère cheese, the Worcestershire sauce and crumbled bacon.

Preheat grill to high. Ladle the soup into bowls and top with bread and remaining cheese. Grill until cheese is melted and toast turns golden. Sprinkle with parsley.

Sweet potato and curry soup

Velvety

If you are lucky enough to be able to buy Kumara – the sweet potato variety more common in New Zealand and Australia – then I would definitely encourage making this soup with it. I personally prefer the flavor of Kumara to the more golden sweet potato variety; however the texture won't be quite so smooth and creamy.

Serves 4

1 Tbsp **olive oil**
1 **onion,** chopped
1 Tbsp **curry powder**
   (mild, medium or hot, depending on taste)
2lb 4oz (1kg) **sweet potatoes,** chopped into chunks
3½ cups (800ml) **chicken stock (see page 12)**
14-fl oz (400-ml) can **coconut milk**
Salt and freshly ground black pepper, to taste

Heat the oil in a large stockpot or saucepan. Add the onion and sauté for 3–4 minutes or until softened but not brown. Add the curry powder and stir to combine before adding the sweet potato. Stir until the sweet potato is evenly coated in oil and curry powder. Add the chicken stock and coconut milk and bring to a boil. Reduce the heat and simmer, uncovered, for about 20 minutes or until the sweet potato is cooked and tender.

Transfer to a blender, in two batches, and purée until smooth. Return to the pan, bring back to a boil, and season with salt and pepper to taste.

▓ *Try using white potatoes, pumpkins or parsnips instead of sweet potatoes if you prefer – they're all delicious.*

Chunky

There are several reasons why certain people are fabulous chunky soup makers: these include a love for hearty comfort foods, patience and the ability to multi-task while the soup is simmering. Some cooks combine all of these.

My mother falls comfortably in the "all of the above" category. Her creations fill the kitchen with aromas that calm and soothe whoever comes into the room. Her soups are usually so packed with goodness they are hearty enough to make a complete meal in themselves – except for a little warm bread, of course.

But not everyone truly understands what a chunky soup means. Take, for example, one evening when Mr. B dropped in on chunky-soup night. He sat down, slathered butter on warm, home-made bread and dipped it into a bowl of tomato and lentil soup. We ate, chatted, and he cleaned his bowl. When my mother asked if he wanted some more, he replied, "Of course not, I have to keep some room for the main course!"

Mr. B missed the beauty of chunky soups. They fill the body and nourish the soul in one, big, easy-to-wash-up bowl.

Black bean soup with salsa and chips
Smoky

Whether at Borough or Portobello Market, cold Saturdays in London for me always meant a bowl of black bean soup with tortillas and salsa from the Cool Chilli Company stall. I make this soup – my version of the original – when I'm feeling chilly.

Serves 6

2 Tbsp **olive oil**
1 **ham hock**
1 **onion,** finely diced
3 **cloves garlic,** finely chopped
1 **chipotle chilli in adobo sauce,** finely chopped
1 **carrot,** finely diced
1 **celery stick,** finely diced
¾ cup (15g) **coriander,** finely chopped
2 tsp **ground cumin**
4½ cups (1.5L) **chicken or vegetable stock** (see pages 12–13)
1 cup (150g) **dried black beans,** soaked overnight and rinsed well
½ tsp **salt**
¼ tsp **pepper**
Juice of 1 **lime**
scant 1 cup (200ml) **crème fraîche or sour cream**
Tomato jalapeño salsa (see page 161)
½ cup (100g) **corn chips**

Heat the olive oil in a stockpot over high heat and add the ham hock. Sauté for 1–2 minutes until slightly browned. Reduce the heat and stir in the onion, garlic, chilli, carrot, celery, coriander and cumin and cook, covered, for about 10 minutes, stirring every now and then. Add the beans, stock, salt and pepper. Cover and simmer, stirring occasionally, for 1½ hours, or until the beans are tender. Remove the ham hock and discard.

Purée half the soup and return to the pot. Reheat gently. Stir in the lime juice. Ladle into bowls and top each bowl with a spoonful of crème fraîche, a spoonful of salsa and a few corn chips.

Black bean soup with salsa and chips

Red onion, chorizo and chickpea soup

Tasty

This soup was devised on the country roads in Normandy while we sat repairing a punctured bicycle tire. Everyone offered their suggestions and this is what I concocted. It's more Italian with a Spanish twist than French, but French-inspired nonetheless.

Serves 4

4 Tbsp **olive oil**
2lb 4oz (1kg) **red onions, about** 6 **medium,** finely sliced
4 **sprigs thyme,** plus extra to garnish
1 tsp **granulated sugar**
5½oz (150g) **chorizo,** cut into small cubes
14-oz (400-g) can **chickpeas,** drained and rinsed
1 Tbsp **tomato purée or paste**
Freshly ground black pepper and **salt** to taste
½ cup (100ml) **Marsala**
4½ cups (1L) **vegetable or pork stock (see page 13)**

Heat the oil in a large saucepan. Add the onions, thyme and sugar and reduce the heat. Cook for 12–15 minutes, stirring very occasionally until the onion begins to caramelize. Add the chorizo and chickpeas and sauté for a further 2–3 minutes. Stir in the tomato purée, season with salt and pepper and increase the heat. Add the Marsala and stir, allowing the alcohol to evaporate. Add the stock, bring back to a boil, and simmer for a further 5–10 minutes. Garnish with extra thyme leaves and serve.

■ *Brown onions can be used instead of red onions.*

Chickpea, garlic and coriander soup

Intricate

This flavorsome soup is neither smooth nor chunky, but it is definitely hearty. Soaking the chickpeas, toasting the spices and using six fat cloves of garlic bring this soup alive.

Serves 6

1 Tbsp **coriander seeds**
1 Tbsp **cumin seeds**
2 Tbsp **butter**
6 **cloves garlic,** chopped
1 **long red chilli,** deseeded and chopped
¾ cup (15g) **coriander,** stalks and leaves separated and chopped
1 tsp **ground turmeric**
2 cups (400g) **dried chickpeas,** cooked (see pages 19–20)
6¼ cups (1.5L) **chicken or vegetable stock** (see pages 12–13)
Grated rind of 1 **lemon**
½ tsp **salt**
¼ tsp **pepper**
2–3 Tbsp **lemon juice**
½ cup (100ml) **sour cream or crème fraîche**

Heat a pan and toast the coriander and cumin seeds until they jump. Remove from the heat and crush using a mortar and pestle. Melt the butter in a large saucepan. Add the spices, garlic, chilli and chopped coriander stalks and sauté over medium heat until very fragrant, about 5 minutes. Add the turmeric and stir. Remove from the heat.

Take half the chickpeas and purée with ½ cup (125ml) stock. Add the puréed and whole chickpeas to the pot, together with the lemon rind and remaining stock. Season with salt and pepper and simmer gently for 30 minutes. Just before serving, stir in the lemon juice and sour cream then sprinkle over the chopped coriander leaves.

Mushroom and rice noodle soup

Mushroom and rice noodle soup

Hale

A Spoonful of Ginger, a health-giving book on Oriental food written by friend and food writer Nina Simonds, is my staple. This soup is inspired by Nina.

Serves 6

9-oz (250-g) **packet rice noodles**
10 **dried Chinese black mushrooms**
1 Tbsp **vegetable oil**
1 tsp **sesame oil**
2 **large leeks,** white and pale green parts only, julienned
2 **large carrots,** julienned
3 Tbsp **very finely chopped garlic**
3 Tbsp **very finely chopped fresh ginger**
6 cups (450g) sliced **button mushrooms**
⅔ cup (150ml) **rice wine**

For the broth:
Black mushroom soaking liquid
4½ cups (1L) **chicken stock** (see page 12)
5 Tbsp **soy sauce**
4 Tbsp **oyster sauce**
½ tsp **black pepper**
1 Tbsp **cornstarch**

Soak the noodles in hot water – see the instructions on the packet. Drain when soft.

Soak the Chinese mushrooms in 3 cups (750ml) boiling water for 30 minutes. Drain, reserving the liquid. Discard the stems and slice the caps.

Combine the broth ingredients and set aside.

Heat the oils in a large saucepan over medium-high heat. Add the leeks and carrots and stir-fry for 2 minutes. Add the garlic, ginger, Chinese and button mushrooms and continue to stir-fry until the moisture evaporates, about 3–5 minutes. Add the rice wine and stir-fry for a further minute. Add the broth ingredients to the soup. Divide the noodles between 6 bowls. Ladle over the soup and serve.

Corn chowder with roasted red pepper

Sweet heat

Traditional corn chowder is paired with a piquant pepper topping to create a sweet, yet spicy, toothsome new classic.

Serves 6

2 tsp **olive oil**
2 **onions,** chopped
2 **potatoes,** diced
2 **celery sticks,** chopped
1 **red pepper,** diced
¼ tsp **chilli flakes**
2¼ cups (500ml) **chicken stock (see page 12)**
2 x 10-fl oz (284-ml) cans **creamed sweet corn**
½ cup (100g) **fresh or frozen sweet corn kernels**
½ tsp **salt**
¼ tsp **pepper**

To garnish:
1 **long red chilli pepper,** halved and cored
1 **red pepper,** halved and cored
3 tsp **olive oil**
1 pinch **salt**
1 pinch **pepper**

Preheat the oven to 400°F/200°C.

Heat the olive oil in a large saucepan over medium heat. Add the onions and sauté until golden, about 10 minutes. Add the potatoes, celery, red pepper and chilli flakes. Stir for 1 minute. Add the stock, creamed sweet corn and the fresh or frozen sweet corn kernels and simmer gently until the potatoes are tender, about 20 minutes. Season with salt and pepper.

Meanwhile, place the chilli pepper and halved red pepper in a small baking dish and toss with 1 tsp olive oil. Roast for 20 minutes, or until the peppers begin to char. Transfer the peppers and juices to a blender, add the remaining olive oil, season and purée.

Swirl a spoonful of the purée onto the chowder and serve.

Corn chowder with roasted red pepper

Ham hock, arborio and squash soup

Stalwart

The ham hock, a staple in many soups from the American Southwest, lends a subtle smokiness to this risotto-like soup.

Serves 4–6

1 Tbsp **coriander seeds**
2 Tbsp **olive oil**
1 Tbsp **butter**
1 **large onion,** finely chopped
1 **celery stick,** finely chopped
3 **cloves garlic,** finely chopped
½ tsp **chilli flakes**
1 handful **coriander,** stalks and leaves separated and chopped
1 **butternut squash,** deseeded and chopped
½ cup (10g) **sage leaves,** finely chopped
½ cup (125ml) **white wine**
1lb 2oz (500g) **ham hock**
6¼ cups (1.5L) **chicken stock** (see page 12)
½ cup (100g) uncooked **arborio rice**
Salt to taste

Heat the coriander seeds in a dry frying pan over medium-high heat until the seeds begin to jump. Remove from the heat and crush the seeds using a mortar and pestle. Set aside.

Heat the oil and butter in a large pan over medium heat. Add the onion and celery, and cook, stirring often until soft, about 5 minutes. Add the garlic, chilli flakes, coriander stalks, squash and sage and stir until fragrant, about 3 minutes. Add the wine and stir until bubbles subside. Add the ham hock and stock and stir. Bring to a boil, cover and simmer for 1 hour. Stir in rice, cover and simmer for 20 minutes or until the rice is tender.

Remove the ham hock from the soup with a slotted spoon. Cut the ham away from the bone, chop and return to pan. Discard bone. Simmer for a few minutes more. Add salt to taste. Garnish with coriander leaves and serve immediately.

Meatball, fennel and tomato soup

Aniseedy

This soup is based on a pasta sauce developed by Rose Gray and Ruth Rogers from the River Café in London.

Serves 4

3½ cups (1kg) **cherry tomatoes**
2 **red onions,** cut into thin wedges
2 tsp **fennel seeds**
2 Tbsp **olive oil**
Sea salt and black pepper
5½oz (150g) **ground lamb**
5½oz (150g) **bulk sausage**
½ cup (30g) **grated Parmesan cheese**
1 cup (20g) **fresh basil leaves,** shredded
generous 1 cup (250ml) **vegetable or lamb stock (see page 13)**
½ cup (100g) **mascarpone**
Extra Parmesan cheese shavings to serve

Preheat the oven to 400°/200°C. Put the cherry tomatoes, onions, fennel seeds and 1 Tbsp of the olive oil in a roasting dish. Season the tomatoes generously with sea salt and black pepper. Roast for 20–25 minutes or until the tomatoes are bursting and the onions are cooked. Set aside to cool.

For the meatballs, combine the ground lamb, bulk sausage, the Parmesan and half of the basil. Season and stir. Shape the lamb mixture into small meatballs, using 1 tsp of mixture per meatball. Heat the remaining oil in a non-stick frying pan and sauté the meatballs until golden and cooked through. Cook in batches. Remove the meatballs from the pan leaving any oil or fat behind.

Add the rest of the basil leaves to the pan and sauté for 10–15 seconds until crispy. Blend the cooled tomato mixture and transfer to a medium saucepan. Add the stock and bring to a boil. Add the mascarpone and browned meatballs. Simmer for 5 minutes then serve with Parmesan shavings and the sautéed basil leaves.

Farro, pancetta and fresh herb soup

Hearty

This is a cherished recipe given to me by my Aunt Betsy. She substitues farro for lentils, depending on what's at hand.

Serves 4–6

3 Tbsp **olive oil**
1 **onion**, finely chopped
1 **celery stick,**
   finely chopped
2 **large carrots,**
   finely chopped
3 **cloves garlic,**
   finely chopped
1 **handful parsley,** stalks
   and leaves separated
   and stalks chopped
1 small bunch **thyme,** finely
   chopped
1 small bunch **rosemary,**
   finely chopped
2¼-oz (60-g) **piece pancetta,**
   finely chopped
14-oz (400-g) can **stewed**
   tomatoes
1 tsp **extra-fine sugar**
1 tsp **dried oregano**
½ tsp **salt**
5 **twists of the pepper mill**
1 cup (200g) **farro**
6¼ cups (1.5L) **chicken or**
   vegetable stock (see
   pages 12–13)
Grated Parmesan cheese

Heat the oil in a large saucepan over medium heat and add the onion. Sauté for 2–3 minutes until the onion becomes translucent. Then, over high heat, add the celery and carrots and continue stirring until the vegetables become brightly colored and slightly tender. Add the garlic, parsley stalks, thyme, rosemary and pancetta and stir until the pancetta slightly browns. Add the tomatoes and their juice, sugar, dried oregano, salt, and pepper. Simmer for 15 minutes, uncovered, stirring occasionally.

Add the farro, stir, then add the stock. Cover and cook slowly until the farro is tender, 30–40 minutes. Add more salt and pepper to taste and serve sprinkled with grated Parmesan and reserved parsley leaves.

Farro, pancetta and fresh herb soup

Minestrone

Minestrone

Wholesome

This soup is an extension of our Vegetable soup (see page 45). A minestrone is a traditional Italian vegetable soup cooked in a meaty stock. The ingredients vary from region to region, depending on the season and what ingredients are available. What all versions have in common is the long, slow manner in which the soup is cooked. Our version is made with beef stock and cannellini beans.

Serves 6

Vegetable soup (see page 45), made using
  beef stock (see page 13)
14-oz (400-g) can **cannellini beans,** drained and rinsed
1½ cups (30g) **fresh basil leaves**
5 Tbsp **grated Parmesan cheese**

Make the vegetable soup. After the soup has simmered for 2½ hours, stir in the cannellini beans.

When you are ready to serve, roughly tear the basil leaves and add to the soup together with the grated Parmesan cheese.

■ *You could use dried beans instead of canned. Soak them overnight, rinse well, then add them to the soup with the stock (see pages 19–20).*

Miso and udon noodle soup
Cleansing

This Japanese soup is not only delicious but it is also exceptionally good for you. You will find the ingredients in specialist Asian grocery stores or in the international section of the supermarket.

Serves 4

2 Tbsp **vegetable oil**
1 tsp **sesame oil**
12oz (350g) **block tofu,** cubed
8 **baby leeks,** sliced thinly on the diagonal
1 tsp **salt**
5 cups (1.2L) **water**
1 Tbsp **miso paste**
1 Tbsp **dashi granules**
1 Tbsp **soy sauce**
Juice of 2 limes
1 Tbsp **fish sauce**
14oz (450g) **"straight to wok" udon noodles**
1 Tbsp **sesame seeds,** toasted
1 cup (20g) **crispy seaweed or nori flakes**

Heat 1 Tbsp of the vegetable oil and the sesame oil in a small non-stick frying pan. Add the tofu and toss to coat. Fry until golden, then remove with a slotted spoon and drain on kitchen paper. Add the sliced leeks and salt to the same pan with the remaining vegetable oil and stir-fry until golden and crispy. Remove the leeks with a slotted spoon and drain on paper towels.

Put the water, miso paste, dashi granules, soy sauce, lime juice and fish sauce in a large saucepan and bring to a boil. Add the noodles and cook as directed on the packet. Stir in half of the leeks and divide between four bowls. Top with the tofu, sesame seeds, the remaining leeks and crispy seaweed before serving.

■ *Try using other types of noodles – rice, ramen and egg noodles are all great substitutes.*

Miso and udon noodle soup

Roasted ratatouille soup

Sumptuous

Ratatouille is basically a ragoût of eggplant, tomatoes, zucchini and peppers. I have added just a bit more liquid and turned this rich vegetable dish into a soup. This soup can be eaten cold, as can the dish it originates from.

Serves 4

1¾ cups (500g) **cherry tomatoes**, halved
1 **medium eggplant** about 10oz (300g), **cut into ⅝-in (1.5-cm) cubes**
2 **zucchini** about 1lb 2oz (500g), cut lengthways into quarters then into ⅝-in (1.5-cm) pieces
1 **red onion**, cut into thin wedges
2 Tbsp **olive oil**
Sea salt and freshly ground black pepper
2 **red peppers**, roasted, skinned and cut into thin strips (see page 19)
2¼ cups (500ml) **vegetable or chicken stock (see pages 12–13)**
2¼ cups (500ml) **tomato juice**
1 **large handful fresh basil leaves**, torn
Extra virgin olive oil, to serve

Preheat the oven to 400°F/200°C.

Put the tomatoes, eggplant, zucchini and red onion in a large roasting pan and drizzle over the olive oil. Toss well to coat evenly, then season generously with sea salt and freshly ground black pepper. Roast for 25–30 minutes, stirring occasionally. When cooked, stir through the sliced red peppers.

Heat the stock and tomato juice together in a large saucepan until near boiling. Add the vegetables and bring to a boil. Reduce the heat and simmer for a further 10–15 minutes. Add most of the torn basil leaves, stir, and serve topped with an extra sprinkling of basil, freshly ground black pepper and a drizzle of your finest extra virgin olive oil.

White bean, lemon and spinach soup

Citrus

To me this soup is typically Italian – white beans, lemon, garlic, and the finest extra virgin olive oil. Spinach adds color but it can be omitted if you prefer.

Serves 4

1½ Tbsp **butter**
1½ Tbsp **olive oil**
1 **onion,** finely chopped
2 **fennel bulbs,** finely chopped
3 **bay leaves**
1 tsp **salt**
Black pepper
Grated rind of 1 **lemon**
4½ cups (1L) **chicken or vegetable stock (see pages 12–13)**
10-oz (300-g) can **cannellini or butter beans,** drained and rinsed
5½oz (150g) **fresh spinach**

To serve:
Crusty ciabatta (Italian bread) loaf
2 **cloves garlic**
Extra virgin olive oil

Heat the butter and olive oil together in a large saucepan or stockpot. Add the onion, fennel and bay leaves and sauté over medium heat for 5–6 minutes or until the onion is translucent and starting to caramelize. Add the salt and season generously with black pepper before adding the lemon rind and stock. Bring to a boil, then add the beans. Reduce the heat to a simmer for 10 minutes while you prepare the bread.

Cut four ¾-in (2-cm) slices of ciabatta and toast under a preheated grill until golden. Peel the garlic cloves, cut in half and rub generously over the bread slices. Drizzle with a little extra virgin olive oil, then place one piece in the bottom of each bowl. Stir the spinach into the soup, allowing it to wilt but still retain its green color. Ladle the soup into the bowls, on top of the bread, and serve with the remaining ciabatta (if you want) and another drizzle of oil.

Smoked fish chowder

Smoked fish chowder

Chunky

This thick and creamy chowder is the ultimate in comfort food. I always go for the option of choosing undyed smoked fish if I can. I find the lurid yellow color of dyed smoked fish a little off-putting.

Serves 4–6

4¾ cups (1L) **milk**
4 **sprigs parsley**
1 tsp **black peppercorns**
2 **dried chillies**
1lb 5oz (600g) **fillets firm smoked fish (cod, haddock or hake)**
¾ stick (100g) **butter**
1 **onion, finely chopped**
1lb 2oz (500g) **potatoes, chopped into ½-in (1-cm) cubes**
3 Tbsp **flour**
generous 1 cup (250ml) **white wine**
Sea salt and freshly ground black pepper
3 Tbsp **chopped parsley**

Put the milk, parsley, peppercorns and chillies in a large heavy-based saucepan and bring to a boil. Reduce the heat to a simmer and add the fish fillets. Simmer for 3–4 minutes until the fish is cooked and flaky. Turn off the heat and remove the fish from the milk. Strain the milk and discard the black peppercorns, chilli and parsley.

Return the pan to the heat and add the butter. When the butter is sizzling, add the onion and potato and sauté for 3–4 minutes. Add the flour and stir to combine. Add the wine, stirring constantly, and allow to bubble. Still stirring, pour the milk into the pan and bring back to a boil. Reduce to a simmer and stir occasionally until thickened, about 6–8 minutes. Flake the fish and return to the pan, seasoning with salt and pepper to taste. Just before serving, stir in the chopped parsley and ladle into warmed bowls.

Spring vegetable and pancetta soup
Fresh

Fresh spring vegetables are a luxury that is only available for a limited period in the year. Get them at their prime and this soup will be sweet, succulent and delicious. Pancetta adds a slight saltiness, which makes for the perfect balance, although it can be omitted for a vegetarian version.

Serves 4

2 Tbsp **olive oil**
7oz (200g) **pancetta**, cubed
1 **onion**, finely sliced
1 **clove garlic**, crushed
1 **pinch chilli flakes**
5 cups (1.2L) **vegetable stock** (see page 13)
2¼ cups (500g) **mashed potatoes**
½ cup (150g) **shelled peas**
9oz (250g) **asparagus**, chopped into ¾-in (2-cm) pieces
¾ cup (150g) **shelled broad beans, or snap peas**, halved
scant 1 cup (200g) **mascarpone**, half in soup and half to garnish
½ cup (10g) **fresh tarragon**, shredded

Heat the oil in a large saucepan or stockpot. Add the pancetta and sauté until golden and cooked. Remove from the pan using a slotted spoon and drain on kitchen paper. Add the onion, garlic and chilli flakes to the pancetta oil and sauté for 3–4 minutes. Add the stock and mashed potato and bring to a boil. Add the peas, asparagus and broad beans and reduce the heat to a simmer. Continue to simmer for a further 6–8 minutes. Stir in the pancetta, mascarpone and tarragon and serve immediately, topped with an extra dollop of mascarpone.

◼ *Use mint instead of tarragon if preferred.*

Spring vegetable and pancetta soup

Tuscan bean soup with parsley pesto

Tuscan bean soup with parsley pesto

Hearty

No one makes a Tuscan bean soup better than our good friend Ursula Ferrigno. However, this one's not bad either. It's a soup full of substance that can only leave you feeling satisfied. Serve with Grissini (see page 154).

Serves 4

2 Tbsp **olive oil**
1 **onion,** finely diced
2 **cloves garlic,**
   finely chopped
2 **celery sticks,** finely diced
2 **carrots,** finely diced
1 **leek,** finely diced
½ tsp **chilli flakes**
2 Tbsp **tomato purée**
1 cup (200g) **dried**
   cannellini beans, cooked
   (see pages 19–20)
14-oz (400-g) can
   chopped tomatoes
1 tsp **extra-fine sugar**
2¼ cups (500ml) **vegetable**
   or chicken stock (see
   pages 12–13)
Salt and black pepper
Parsley pesto
   (see page 158)

Begin by making a *soffritto* (see page 9): heat the oil in a large saucepan or stockpot and add the onion. Sauté for 2–3 minutes until the onion becomes translucent. Add the garlic and stir. Then, over high heat, add the celery, carrots and leek and continue stirring until the vegetables become brightly colored and slightly tender. Add the chilli flakes and tomato purée and stir to combine. Reduce the heat and add the beans, tomatoes, sugar and stock. Bring to a boil, reduce the heat and simmer for 20–30 minutes. Season.

While the soup is simmering, make the parsley pesto. This soup is best if left until the following day as the flavor develops. Serve the hot soup in bowls, topped with 1–2 Tbsp of the pesto, to be stirred in before eating.

Smooth

Smooth soups are rather like ugly ducklings turned into swans. They can begin life as a bulbous butternut squash, a gnarled celeriac or a lumpy chickpea. But after time, care and a little touch of kitchen magic, they are transformed into luxurious beauties.

Kitchen magic comes in many forms. In the case of smooth soups, it manifests itself in a good peeler, a knife, a mouli-légumes, blender, food processor, hand-held blender or sieve.

My grandmother used to say that all you needed when making smooth soup was ingenuity and the basement stairs: every autumn pumpkins would take flight and land in pieces on the basement floor. She would collect the remnants, place them on a chopping board, and peel away with ease and grace.

Smooth soups are a wonderful way to mask the truth. Pumpkins can be smashed. Vegetables can be overcooked. Mushy lentils are forgiven. Unpopular ingredients are blended and concealed. Once puréed, all that is left is flavor and mystery.

Broccoli, yogurt and stilton soup

Sharp

I almost think this soup should have made it into the Classic chapter, as it is a favorite among many. Yogurt is the perfect foil to balance the blue Stilton but I know some people prefer to use heavy cream – it's up to you.

Serves 4

1 Tbsp **olive oil**
1 **onion**, finely diced
½ tsp **chilli flakes** (optional)
2 cups (500g) **broccoli florets**
4½ cups (1L) **vegetable stock** (see page 13)
Juice of ½ **lemon**
1⅔ cups (100g) **fresh bread crumbs**
1¼ cups (300ml) **plain unsweetened yogurt**
1-1¼ cups (100–150g) crumbled **Stilton cheese**, to taste
Freshly ground black pepper
¾ cup (75g) **flaked almonds**, toasted, to garnish

Heat the oil in a large saucepan or stockpot. Add the onion and chilli flakes, if using, and sauté until the onion is translucent. Add the broccoli and sauté for a further minute. Add the stock and lemon juice and bring to a boil. Reduce the heat and simmer for 6–8 minutes or until the broccoli is very tender.

Remove from the heat, add the bread crumbs and purée in batches in a blender until smooth. Return to the saucepan, add the yogurt and Stilton and bring back to a boil. Season with black pepper to taste. Serve topped with toasted flaked almonds.

■ *This is delicious made with cauliflower instead of broccoli, or even a combination of both.*

Carrot soup with dill pesto

Fresh

Carrots, nature's naturally sweet vegetable, combine successfully with many ingredients. Here we've introduced them to the salty, crunchy, fresh flavors of feta cheese, pine nuts and dill. It's happiness all around.

Serves 4

2 Tbsp **butter**
1 **large onion, chopped**
4 **large carrots, chopped**
½ tsp **dill seeds**
5 cups (1.2L) **chicken or vegetable stock (see pages 12–13)**
1 tsp **salt**
Dill pesto (see page 157)

Melt the butter in a large saucepan over medium-low heat. Add the onion and sauté until soft, 5–7 minutes. Add the carrots and dill seeds and sauté for a further 8–10 minutes. Pour in the stock, add salt and bring to a boil. Reduce the heat and simmer, stirring occasionally, for 20 minutes.

Purée until smooth and return to the pan. Gently reheat and divide between bowls. Serve with a spoonful of pesto stirred through each bowl of soup.

Canadian Cheddar and lager soup

Sharp

This soup is based on a recipe given to me by my brother-in-law James. I was skeptical at first – Cheddar and beer are two of Canada's finest ingredients, but together, in a soup? I was wrong to hesitate. They're a match made in, well, Canada.

Serves 4

2 Tbsp **olive oil**
1 Tbsp **butter**
1 **onion, chopped**
1 **large carrot, chopped**
2 **celery sticks, chopped**
2 Tbsp **flour**
1 Tbsp **Dijon mustard**
4½ cups (1L) **chicken stock**
  (see page 12)
1½ cups (350ml) **flat lager**
¾ cup (100g) grated **mature Cheddar cheese**
2 Tbsp **grated Parmesan cheese**
½ tsp **Worcestershire sauce**
Chopped parsley, to
  garnish
Rarebit (see page 156),
  to serve

Melt the olive oil and butter in a large saucepan over medium heat. Add the onion and cook, stirring occasionally, until soft, but not browned. Add the carrot and celery and continue to cook until soft. Stir in the flour and mustard and cook for 3 minutes. Add the stock and lager and simmer for 10 minutes. Purée the soup until smooth.

Before serving, add the cheeses and Worcestershire sauce and stir until the cheese has melted. Garnish with chopped parlsey and serve with rarebit.

Canadian Cheddar and lager soup

Celeriac, pear and rosemary soup

Celeriac, pear and rosemary soup

Fragrant

I like to serve this sweet, aromatic soup with crispy flatbread
or Grissini (see page 154) rather than warm crusty bread.

Serves 4

1 Tbsp **olive oil**
1 **red onion,** finely chopped
3 **bay leaves**
3 **sprigs rosemary**
1 **clove garlic,** crushed
1lb 10oz (750g) **celeriac,**
   chopped
2 **firm pears,** peeled, cored
   and chopped
Salt and black pepper
5 cups (1.2L) **chicken or
   vegetable stock**
   (see pages 12–13)

For the caramelized pears:
½ stick (50g) **butter**
2 **firm pears,** peeled and
   sliced
½ tsp **grated fresh ginger**
1 Tbsp **rosemary needles**

Heat the oil in a large
saucepan or stockpot. Add
the onion, bay leaves and
rosemary and sauté until the
onion is translucent. Add the
garlic and sauté for another
minute. Add the celeriac,
pears and salt and pepper
and stir until coated in the
oil. Add the stock and bring
to a boil. Reduce the heat
and simmer for 15–20
minutes, or until celeriac is
tender. Turn off the heat and
allow to stand for 5 minutes.
Remove the bay leaves and
rosemary stalks, leaving
behind any rosemary leaves
that have fallen off. Blend, in
two batches, until smooth.
Sieve.

Return the soup to the pan
and prepare the caramelized
pears. Heat the butter in a
small frying pan until bubbling.
Add the pear slices, ginger and
rosemary needles and toss to
coat. Leave undisturbed for
3–4 minutes or until the
pears start to turn golden
and smell aromatic. Turn
over and cook for a further
3 minutes. Reheat the soup
to boiling point, then serve
topped with a few pieces of
caramelized pear.

Cream of spinach, coconut and nutmeg

Redolent

Trimming what seems like a mountain of spinach is more than worthwhile, we promise! This soup is best the day it's made.

Serves 6

2 Tbsp **butter**
1 Tbsp **olive oil**
2 **onions, chopped**
1 **celery stick, chopped**
2 x 1lb 2-oz (500-g) bags **fresh spinach, trimmed**
1 tsp **salt**
4½ cups (1L) **vegetable stock (see page 13)**
3½oz (100g) **creamed coconut**
generous 1 cup (250ml) **half-and-half, plus** a little extra to serve
1 tsp **grated fresh nutmeg**
½ tsp **ground black pepper**
Few **peppercorns**, cracked
Grissini (see page 154), to serve

Heat the butter and olive oil in a large pot over medium-low heat. Add the onions and celery and sweat until soft, about 10 minutes. Add the spinach in batches (it will shrink down as it cooks). Reduce the heat to low, sprinkle with salt, stir, cover and cook for 5 minutes.

Purée the spinach and onions in batches with a ladleful of stock each time. Return to the pot and add the remaining stock, creamed coconut, half-and-half, nutmeg and pepper. Taste for seasoning, adding more salt if desired.

Serve with a swirl of half-and-half and a sprinkling of cracked black pepper, with grissini on the side.

■ *Creamed coconut is available in Oriental grocery shops and in many supermarkets.*

■ *Buy whole nutmeg and grate it yourself. Ground nutmeg has only a fraction of the aroma and flavor of its former, whole self.*

Cream of spinach, coconut and nutmeg

Fennel soup with orange gremolata

Fennel soup with orange gremolata

Aniseed

Gremolata is an Italian garnish of parsley, garlic and lemon rind, traditionally sprinkled over *osso buco*. Here we take it to another level, substituting orange rind for lemon and pairing it with a velvety fennel soup – a fresh, inspired combination.

Serves 4

1 Tbsp **butter**
1 Tbsp **olive oil**
2 **leeks,** whites and pale green parts only, chopped
2 **onions,** chopped
1 **clove garlic,** crushed
1 **fennel bulb,** chopped and fronds reserved for the gremolata
⅔ cup (150ml) **white wine**
3½ cups (800ml) **chicken or vegetable stock (see pages 12–13)**
¼ tsp **salt**
¼ tsp **pepper**
¼ tsp **nutmeg**
generous 1 cup (250ml) **half-and-half**
2 tsp **Pernod**
Orange gremolata (see page 157)

Heat the butter and olive oil over medium heat in a large stockpot. Add the leeks, onions, garlic and fennel, and sauté, stirring occasionally, for 15 minutes. Add the wine, bring to a boil and simmer until the liquid evaporates. Add the stock, salt, pepper and nutmeg. Simmer for 10 minutes until the vegetables are very soft.

Purée the soup until smooth and return to the pot. Reheat gently. Stir in the cream and Pernod before serving. Divide the soup between four bowls. Top each bowl with a spoonful of gremolata.

Moroccan spiced carrot soup

Aromatic

Jennifer Joyce and Victoria Blashford-Snell, from the London bookshop Books for Cooks, make delicious Moroccan spiced carrots in their book *Diva Cooking*. We've turned their recipe into a soup and added an extra garnish of crispy shallots.

Serves 4

1½ tsp **cumin seeds**
1½ tsp **coriander seeds**
1 Tbsp **sesame seeds**
1 Tbsp **smoked sweet Spanish paprika**
2 Tbsp **olive oil**
1 **onion,** finely chopped
2 **cloves garlic,** finely chopped
4½ cups (700g) **chopped carrots**
3 Tbsp **red wine vinegar**
1 tsp **salt**
4½ cups (1L) **chicken stock** (see page 12)
Crispy shallots (see page 152)
½ cup (100ml) **plain unsweetened yogurt,** to garnish (optional)

Toast the cumin, coriander and sesame seeds in a small dry frying pan until lightly golden and aromatic. Transfer to a spice grinder (or mortar and pestle) and grind with the paprika to a fine powder.

Heat the oil in a large stockpot and add the onion. Sauté until translucent then add the garlic, carrots and spice mix. Stir to coat and sauté for a further 2 minutes. Add the vinegar and allow to bubble away before adding the salt and stock. Bring to a boil, reduce the heat and simmer for 15–20 minutes or until carrots are tender. (While the soup is simmering, prepare the crispy shallots.)

Turn off heat and allow soup to cool for 5 minutes. Blend, in two batches, until smooth. Return to the pan and bring back to a boil before stirring in half of the crispy shallots. Serve sprinkled with the remaining garnish and a dollop of yogurt if you like.

Moroccan spiced carrot soup

Roasted garlic and onion soup
Nourishing

Although this soup is not the most attractive of colors, the addition of red chicory looks fantastic and the extra sprig of thyme when serving adds a touch of elegance.

Serves 4

2 Tbsp **olive oil**
4 **red onions,** unpeeled
1 **large head garlic (about 10 cloves),** unpeeled
1 **red chilli,** deseeded and finely chopped
1 **small bunch thyme**
6¼ cups (1.5 L) **vegetable stock (see page 13)**
2 cups (200g) **chopped potatoes**

To serve:
2 **heads red chicory**
1 Tbsp **olive oil**
1 tsp **balsamic vinegar**
4 **thyme sprigs**

Preheat the oven to 400°F/200°C. Put 1 Tbsp oil and the onions in a roasting pan, toss and roast for 30 minutes. Add the garlic head and roast for a further 30 minutes or until the onions and garlic are soft. Peel and chop the onions and squeeze the garlic from their skins.

Heat the remaining 1 Tbsp oil in a large saucepan or stockpot. Add the onion, garlic, chilli and thyme. Sauté for 2–3 minutes. Add the stock and potato and bring to a boil. Reduce the heat and simmer for about 30 minutes. Blend, in two batches, until smooth. Return to the pan and stir until heated through.

While the soup is reheating, cut the chicory heads into quarters lengthwise. Heat the oil and balsamic vinegar in a shallow frying pan, then add the chicory. Sauté for 2–3 minutes, turning occasionally, until softened and golden. To serve, ladle the soup into bowls and top with a couple of pieces of chicory and a sprig of thyme.

Squash, potato and peanut butter soup

Velvety

Peanut butter may seem an unlikely ingredient to feature in a soup, but paired with velvety smooth autumn vegetables it makes for a glorious combination.

Serves 6

1 **butternut squash, about** 2lb 4oz (1kg)
1 **large sweet potato, chopped**
4 Tbsp **butter**
½ cup (125ml) **smooth unsweetened peanut butter**
4½ cups (1L) **vegetable stock (see page 13)**
1 tsp **grated fresh nutmeg**
1 Tbsp **runny honey**
1 tsp **salt**
½ tsp **black pepper**

Preheat the oven to 350°F/180°C.

Cut the squash into quarters. Scoop out the seeds and stringy flesh and discard. Place the quarters flesh-side down on a baking pan and roast for 1 hour or until soft. Remove from oven and cool.

Place the sweet potato in a saucepan, cover with cold water and boil until tender. Drain off the water and purée. The purée should yield about 1¼ cups (300g).

When the squash has cooled, scoop out the flesh with a spoon and purée. This purée should yield about 2½ cups (600g).

Heat the butter in a large saucepan. Add the puréed squash, sweet potato and peanut butter. Stir to combine. Add the stock, nutmeg, honey, salt and pepper. Simmer gently for 10–15 minutes. If the soup is too thick, thin with more stock. Taste for seasoning and serve.

■ *It is important to use unsweetened peanut butter in this recipe – sweetened varieties would overpower the soup.*

Thai pumpkin soup

Creamy

If I had to name the meal I ate most frequently while a university student, this would be it. Served with big chunks of crusty bread, it was the perfect student food. It's cheap and easy to make and freezes well too – and everyone loves it!

Serves 4

1 Tbsp **olive oil**
5 **shallots,** sliced
1 **clove garlic,** finely chopped
1 **red chilli,** deseeded and chopped
½oz (15g) **fresh ginger,** grated
2lb 12oz (1.25kg) **pumpkin,** deseeded and chopped
14-fl oz (400-ml) **coconut milk**
2¼ cups (500ml) **chicken stock (see page 12)**
¾ cup (15g) **fresh coriander,** plus extra to garnish
Salt to taste

Heat the oil in a large saucepan or stockpot. Add the shallots, garlic, chilli and ginger and sauté for 3–4 minutes, or until sweated but not browned. Add the pumpkin and stir to coat in oil. Add the coconut milk and stock, stir and bring to a boil. Reduce the heat and simmer for about 20 minutes or until the pumpkin is tender. Turn off the heat and stir in the coriander.

Transfer to a blender or food processor in two batches and purée until smooth. Taste, and add a little salt if needed. Return to the pan and bring back to a boil. Garnish with some extra coriander and serve.

■ *Serve this with a spoonful of Coconut sambal (see page 152) on top if you're feeling extravagant.*

Thai pumpkin soup

Chilled

Cravings are curious things. Sometimes it's a flavor we're after. At other times it's texture. For us, it's also a particular action, such as the twirling of spaghetti, the lifting of sushi with chopsticks, the pulling apart of warm cinnamon rolls, and the slurp of soup from a spoon. And when the urge strikes, we have to act.

That's how the cold soup passion began. It wasn't a cold, wintry day, but spoon to mouth was what we craved. Melons were blended with mint and swirled with yogurt. Peaches were blended with sparkling wine and topped with cream. Rhubarb was sweetened and simmered with mango, and red beets were spiced and stirred with cool cream.

Cold soup isn't an original idea. Legend has it that sometime in the early 1900s, the chef at the Ritz Carlton Hotel in New York hailed from Vichy in France. One day he forgot to heat the leek and potato soup he had planned to serve at the opening of the hotel's roof garden. In a panic, he added fresh cream and chives, and voilà, Vichyssoise was born. A happy, cool accident.

Cucumber soup with smoked trout
Soothing

A gentle cooking, contrary to the usual practice with most chilled cucumber soups, adds depth and flavor to this delicious summer soup.

Serves 6

1 Tbsp **butter**
¾ cup (100g) **chopped onion**
4 **cucumbers**, peeled, halved, deseeded and chopped
1 **potato**, chopped
3½ cups (800ml) **vegetable stock (see page 13)**
¾ cup (15g) **dill**, stalks and fronds separated and chopped
1 tsp **salt**
generous 1 cup (250ml) **sour cream**
5½oz (150g) **smoked trout** chopped

Melt the butter in a heavy bottomed saucepan over medium-low heat. Add the onion and sauté until soft, about 5 minutes. Stir in the cucumbers and potato and sauté for a further minute. Add the stock, dill stalks and salt. Bring to a boil, then simmer until the potato is tender, about 20 minutes. Purée the soup until smooth. Cool. Stir in ⅔ cup (150ml) of the sour cream and the dill fronds. Cover and chill in the fridge until cold, 3–4 hours.

Serve with a dollop of the remaining sour cream and a sprinkling of chopped smoked trout.

■ *Substitute smoked salmon for the trout if preferred.*

Iced red beet soup

Earthy

This soup is quick and simple to make if you use store-bought, ready-cooked red beets. However, if time is available then there is nothing more satisfying than roasting your own beetroot (see page 21).

Serves 6–8

14oz (400g) **can store-bought pre-cooked red beets, or roast your own**
1 Tbsp **balsamic vinegar**
1 tsp **horseradish cream**
1 **small onion,** grated
3 cups (700ml) **Greek yogurt,** plus extra to serve
Salt and freshly ground black pepper
1½ cups (300ml) **orange juice or iced water** (optional)

To serve:
6–8 ice cubes
4 Tbsp Greek yogurt

Put the red beets, balsamic vinegar, horseradish cream, onion, yogurt and seasoning into a blender or food processor and blend until smooth. Add as much orange juice or iced water as you like, depending on the desired consistency. Transfer to a bowl and refrigerate for at least 2 hours until well chilled.

Serve over ice cubes with a dollop of Greek yogurt.

■ *Red beets and ginger are great friends. Try adding 1 Tbsp of grated fresh ginger in place of the horseradish for a different flavor.*

Avocado and cucumber soup

Luxurious

I had a similar soup to this at one of Terence Conran's restaurants in London. Here it is served with a wasabi salsa. I would suggest serving this soup in small amounts, as it's rich, creamy and very filling.

Serves 6–8

4 **ripe avocados,** halved, stoned and peeled
Juice of 2 **limes**
½ **cucumber,** about 6oz (175g), roughly chopped
1 **clove garlic**
2¼ cups (500ml) **chicken stock (see page 12),** cold
⅔ cup (150ml) **sour cream** (optional)
Freshly ground black pepper

For the salsa:
3½oz (100g) **cucumber,** deseeded and finely diced
2 **tomatoes,** deseeded and finely diced
1 **small red onion,** finely chopped
2–3 Tbsp **extra virgin olive oil**
¼ cup (5g) **fresh coriander,** chopped
1–2 tsp **wasabi** or to taste
Salt and freshly ground black pepper

Put all the soup ingredients except the black pepper in a blender or food processor and blend until smooth. Add pepper to taste and place in the fridge for about 2 hours or until well chilled.

Make the salsa. Combine all the ingredients except the wasabi, salt and pepper in a small bowl. Add wasabi and salt and pepper to taste. Serve the soup in small bowls – or shot glasses if serving it as a canapé – with a little salsa spooned on top.

Avocado and cucumber soup

Gazpacho

Gazpacho

Textured

Gazpacho is a classic Spanish chilled soup featuring various vegetables, notably tomato, cucumber and garlic. Its consistency can vary from very liquid to chunky to almost solid. We like a gazpacho somewhere in the middle, but feel free to adjust the texture to your liking.

Serves 6–8

1 cucumber, unpeeled
  and deseeded
1 lb 5oz (600g) tomatoes,
  skinned (see page 19)
  and deseeded
1 large red pepper,
  deseeded and chopped
1 red onion, chopped
1 large red chilli, deseeded
  and chopped
2 cloves garlic
2 Tbsp tomato paste
Salt and freshly ground
  black pepper
1 bunch basil or marjoram,
  about ¾ cup (15g)
2½ cups (600ml) good-
  quality tomato juice
3 Tbsp extra virgin olive oil
2 Tbsp sherry vinegar or
  red wine vinegar

To serve:
Basil oil (see page 21)
4-in (10-cm) piece
  cucumber, deseeded
  and finely diced
½ red pepper, finely diced
Basil leaves (optional)

Put all the soup ingredients except the tomato juice, oil and vinegar in a food processor. While processing, pour in the tomato juice through the funnel followed by the oil and vinegar. Taste and season accordingly, then cover and chill.

To serve, pour into small glasses or bowls and drizzle over some basil oil. Sprinkle with a few chopped cucumber and red pepper pieces and finish with a basil leaf if you want. Season and serve immediately.

Smoked eggplant and thyme soup

Complex

I came across the wonderful smoky flavor of grilled eggplants in a Celia Brooks Brown Thai cooking class at London's Books for Cooks.

Serves 4–6

3 slender eggplants
2 Tbsp **olive oil**
1 **large onion**, chopped
1 **shallot**, very finely chopped
2 **cloves garlic**, very finely
   chopped
1 **chipotle chilli in adobo
   sauce**, chopped
3–4½ cups (750ml–1L)
   **chicken stock (see
   page 12)**
1 cup (20g) **thyme sprigs**
generous 1 cup (250ml)
   half-and-half
½ tsp **salt**
¼ tsp **black pepper**
Heavy cream, to garnish

Place the eggplants on a baking tray and put directly under a preheated grill. Turn every few minutes until charred and collapsed. Transfer to a plate and allow to cool. Peel off the skin over a bowl to catch all the flesh and juices. Discard the skin and set the flesh aside.

Heat the olive oil in a large saucepan over medium heat. Add the onion and sauté until translucent. Add the shallots, garlic and chilli and sauté for a further minute. Add the stock and thyme. Bring to a boil, reduce the heat and simmer for 30 minutes until reduced by half.

Stir in the half and half and simmer for a further 3 minutes. Discard the thyme sprigs. Stir in the eggplant flesh, salt and pepper. Remove from the heat and cool slightly. Purée the mixture and return to a cleaned pan. Add a further 1 cup (250ml) stock to thin if necessary.

Serve immediately, or chill and serve cold, garnished with a swirl of heavy cream.

Sorrel soup

Dainty

I was given this recipe by a friend's grandmother, Mary Grant.
Her Nova Scotia garden overlooks the Atlantic Ocean, and in
late summer it is full of sorrel. This delicate yet simple soup is
a chilled version of what usually becomes of her crop.

Serves 4

3oz (80g) **fresh sorrel leaves**
3 Tbsp **butter**
1 **medium onion,** chopped
1 Tbsp **flour**
3 cups (750ml) **chicken stock (see page 12)**
2 **egg yolks,** at room temperature
generous 1 cup (250ml) **half-and-half**
Salt and pepper, to taste
⅔–1 cup (150–200ml) **crème fraîche**

Trim the sorrel leaves from stems and veins. Rinse and pat dry.
Melt the butter in a large saucepan over low heat. Add the onions
and sweat until translucent. Add the flour and sorrel and stir. Cook
over low heat until the leaves are wilted. Stir in stock and simmer
for 2–3 minutes.

Purée the soup until smooth, pour through a sieve and return
soup to a clean saucepan over low heat.

In a medium-sized bowl beat the egg yolks. Stir in the half-and-
half. Slowly temper the eggs by whisking in 1 cup (250ml) of soup
to the egg mixture. Pour the egg mixture back into the pan with
the rest of the soup (this will stop the eggs from curdling), season
and simmer for a further 2–3 minutes.

Cool and then chill. Taste for seasoning. Serve with a dollop of
crème fraîche.

Red pepper, paprika and orange soup

Tangy

It is no surprise that roasted peppers and paprika go so well together. Paprika is actually the dried, ground fruits of the mild capsicum pepper, often called pimento. I like to use a sweet variety of paprika and let my discerning guests add a dash of Tabasco if they choose.

Serves 6–8

2 **red peppers**, roasted (see page 19)
4 **medium tomatoes**, skinned (see page 19) and halved
Juice and zest of 1 **orange**
½–1 tsp **sweet paprika**
1 tsp **extra-fine sugar**
2¼ cups (500ml) **ice cold water**
Salt and freshly ground black pepper
Tabasco sauce, to taste (optional)
6–8 **mint ice cubes**, to serve (see page 162)

Put all the ingredients, except the Tabasco sauce and the ice cubes, in a blender and blend until smooth. Pass through a fine sieve or muslin to remove any seeds, and season to taste. Serve with mint ice cubes in small glasses and add a dash of Tabasco sauce if desired.

■ *This soup is also delicious made without the red peppers. Increase the number of tomatoes used to 8 and omit the roasted peppers. You will have a fabulously fragrant chilled tomato soup.*

Red pepper, paprika and orange soup

Thai melon and minted crab soup

Intricate

Sweet and savory come together in this easy yet distinctive colorful soup, which will impress both you and your guests.

Serves 6

1 cantaloupe, deseeded, skinned and chopped
1 stalk lemongrass
1 Tbsp vegetable oil
3 Tbsp finely chopped shallots
2 Tbsp finely chopped fresh ginger
2 cloves garlic, finely chopped
2 lime leaves, deveined and finely chopped
1 small green chilli, deseeded and finely chopped
Juice of 2 limes
½ tsp salt
1lb (450g) crabmeat
1 handful mint leaves, finely chopped
1 handful basil leaves, finely chopped
Pinch salt

Purée the melon and set aside. The yield should be about 6¼ cups (1.5L). Remove the skin from the lemongrass and finely chop the thicker end of the stalk.

Heat the vegetable oil in a large saucepan over medium heat. Add the lemongrass, shallots, ginger, garlic and lime leaves and cook for 5 minutes. Add 2¼ cups (500ml) of melon purée, stir and simmer for a further 5 minutes. Remove from the heat and add the remaining melon purée, together with the chilli, juice of 1 lime and salt. Purée again until smooth, then strain and chill.

Pick over the crabmeat to make sure all the shell has been removed. Toss with mint, basil and juice of the other lime and sprinkle with a pinch of salt.

Divide the crabmeat between the 6 bowls. Ladle soup around it and serve.

Cranberry with crumbled chèvre soup

Fragrant

This is a lovely and very pretty way to end a meal, especially in the autumn when cranberries are in season. Crumbled chèvre makes an intriguing accompaniment to this soup.

Serves 6

5¼ cups (600g) **fresh or frozen cranberries**
1 cup (200g) **extra-fine sugar**
1 Tbsp **lemon zest**
2¼ cups (500ml) **dry white wine**
3 cups (750ml) **water**
2 **cinnamon sticks**
2 **star anise**
4 **cloves**
2 Tbsp **lemon juice**
generous 1 cup (250ml) **half-and-half**

To garnish:
1 cup (100g) crumbled **firm, mild chèvre or feta**

Place the cranberries, sugar, lemon zest, white wine, water, cinnamon, star anise and cloves in a large saucepan. Bring to a boil then simmer for 20–30 minutes stirring occasionally until the cranberries have collapsed.

Sieve the soup into a clean pot, pushing the ingredients through with the back of a spoon. Stir in the lemon juice and half-and-half and heat gently.

Divide between bowls and top with crumbled chèvre.

Melon, mint and basil soup

Refreshing

The inspiration for this recipe comes from my Aunt Sandra, whose creativity and passion for flavor always make for delicious food. It is a calming, pale green soup with a hint of herby freshness – an elegant ending to a summer meal.

Serves 4

1 **honeydew** about 3lb 5oz (1.5kg)
generous 1 cup (250ml) **water**
generous ¼ cup (60g) **extra-fine sugar**
1 cup (20g) **fresh mint**
Juice of ½ **lemon**
1 **small cantaloupe**
1 **handful fresh mint and basil leaves,** finely sliced

Chop the honeydew in half, scoop out the seeds and cut off the skin. Chop the flesh into cubes then purée in batches. Transfer to a large bowl. Make a syrup by combining water, sugar and mint in a small saucepan. Bring to a boil, reduce the heat to low and simmer gently for 5 minutes. Remove from the heat and strain the mixture into the purée. Add the lemon juice and stir. Cover with plastic wrap and chill in the fridge.

Before serving, cut the cantaloupe melon in half and scoop out the seeds. Scoop out the flesh with a melon baller and place the balls in a bowl. Toss with the finely-sliced mint and basil leaves. Divide the melon balls between four bowls and spoon over the soup.

Melon, mint and basil soup

Rhubarb, mango and jasmine soup

Rhubarb, mango and jasmine soup

Exotic

Rhubarb and mango, poached in sweetened jasmine tea, take on a floral quality that will intrigue the taste buds. Serve with edible flower ice cubes or a spoonful of Greek yogurt.

Serves 6

3½ cups (800ml) **water**
3 **jasmine tea bags or** 3 Tbsp **loose jasmine tea leaves** in enclosed strainer
1lb 10oz (750g) **rhubarb,** chopped
1lb 10oz (750g) **mango,** chopped
1¼ cups (250g) **extra-fine sugar**
2 Tbsp **finely chopped fresh ginger**
1 **vanilla pod**
generous 1 cup (250ml) **Greek yogurt,** plus extra to serve if liked
Pansy ice cubes (see page 162)

Bring the water to a boil in a medium-sized saucepan. Add the tea bags, remove from the heat and leave to infuse for 15 minutes. Discard the tea bags. Add the rhubarb, mango, sugar and ginger.

Slit the vanilla pod from top to bottom. Using the top of a small, pointed knife, scrape out the seeds and add to the tea, together with the pod. Bring to a boil, reduce the heat and simmer until the fruit is tender, about 20 minutes.

Remove from the heat and cool slightly. Purée the soup in batches and return to a clean pan. Whisk in 1 cup (250ml) yogurt, cover with plastic wrap and chill. Add pansy ice cubes to serve.

Strawberry and cardamom soup

Aromatic

If you make this soup when strawberries are at their optimum, you will have a deliciously sweet and fragrant result.

Serves 4–6

½ cup (100g) **extra-fine sugar**
scant 1 cup (200ml) **cold water**
4–6 **cardamom pods,** crushed
Zest of 1 **lime**
1lb 2oz (500g) **strawberries,** hulled
scant ½ cup (200g) **crème fraîche or mascarpone**

Put the sugar, water, cardamom and lime zest in a small saucepan and bring to a boil. Reduce the heat and simmer for 10 minutes. Set aside and allow to cool for about 20–30 minutes. Strain the syrup through a fine sieve, reserving the liquid.

Put the strawberries, syrup and crème fraiche in a blender and liquidize until smooth. If you want to get rid of the strawberry seeds, strain the soup again through a fine sieve. Chill for a couple of hours (if you have time) before serving in small glasses topped with extra strawberries slices if you like.

▒ *Add a couple of extra tablespoons of sugar while blending if your strawberries aren't as seasonal and sweet as you would like.*

Peach soup

Effervescent

This soup is best at the end of summer when peaches are perfectly ripe, sweet and juicy. It's also incredibly simple, because with fresh, seasonal fruit soups, the simpler the better. The white wine adds a sophisticated, Bellini-like quality to the soup.

Serves 4–6

6 **ripe peaches**, peeled, stoned and sliced
½ cup (125ml) **peach juice**
10oz (300g) **fresh pineapple**, cut into chunks
½ cup (125ml) **chilled white wine**, still or sparkling
Juice and zest of 1 **lime**

Blend peaches, peach juice and pineapple in a blender or liquidizer. Blend in the wine and lime juice. Strain and chill. Serve with a sprinkling of lime zest curls.

■ *Ripe nectarines can be substituted for peaches in this recipe.*

Spicy

Green chillies are so immature, especially those tiny thin-skinned ones. But it's not their fault; they are picked just three months after being planted. If left alone, they'll mature into yellow, orange, red, brown or purple chillies. Some say they're better that way. Either way, chillies will never kick their fiery side.

Their hot temperament comes from the presence of capsaicin in their seeds, skin and fleshy parts. The amount depends on the variety of chilli and its degree of ripeness. Removing the seeds and veins will weaken the chilli's heat, but won't render it totally innocuous.

Chillies grow in hot climates. You will find them in many parts of Asia, Africa and the American Southwest. They vary in their heat, size, color and texture. They can be as long as your forearm or as tiny as your fingernail. Some are smoked or dried, some are fresh, some are sold in a sauce; others are made into a paste. They are all an excellent source of vitamins A and C. They stimulate circulation and digestion, encourage perspiration and cool the body.

Chilli chicken and brown rice soup

Savory

This really is a one-pot meal: chicken, pumpkin and rice.

Serves 4–6

1 **chicken** about 2lb 4oz (1kg), **giblets removed and chicken rinsed**
2 x 14-fl oz (400-ml) cans **coconut milk**
12 cups (3L) **cold water**
4–6 **dried chillies**
4 **cloves garlic**
6 **dried curry leaves**
¼ cup (40g) **palm sugar**
1 Tbsp **olive oil**
6 **shallots**, finely chopped
1–2 tsp **chilli paste**
Scant 1 cup (200g) **uncooked brown rice**, rinsed
1lb 2oz (500g) **pumpkin**, chopped into ½-in (1-cm) cubes and roasted at 400°F/200°C for about 30 minutes, in 1 Tbsp of olive oil
4 **baby spring onions**, roughly chopped

Put the chicken in a large stockpot. Add 1 can coconut milk and top with cold water until the liquid just covers the chicken. Add the chillies, garlic, curry leaves and palm sugar and bring to a boil. Reduce the heat and simmer for 40 minutes or until the chicken is cooked through. Remove from the liquid and set aside to cool. Sieve the liquid and discard the chillies, garlic and curry leaves. Set aside.

Heat the oil in the same pan. Add the shallots and sauté until translucent. Add the chilli paste and sauté for a further minute. Stir in the rice, then add 5 cups (1.2L) of the stock and the other can of coconut milk. Bring to a boil, then reduce the heat and simmer, uncovered, for 20–25 minutes or until the rice is cooked.

When the chicken is cool enough to handle, shred it into pieces. When the rice is cooked, add the chicken, pumpkin and spring onions to the pan and bring back to a boil. Turn off the heat and leave, covered, for 10 minutes before serving.

Chilli chicken and brown rice soup

Hot and sour fish soup

Piquant

Tom Yum soup is almost as popular with foreigners as it is with the people of Thailand where it originated. If time is limited, then buy a jar of Tom Yum paste or Tom Yum stock cubes from an Oriental supermarket and use this to make the stock. Just add the fish and vegetables of your choice and the soup will be ready in minutes.

Serves 4

6¼ cups (1.5L) **Oriental stock (see page 14)**
generous ¼ cup (50g) **palm sugar,** plus extra if needed
2 Tbsp **fish sauce**
Juice of 1 **lime**
1lb 5oz (600g) **firm white fish (cod or haddock)** cubed
½ cup (10g) **chopped coriander,** plus extra sprigs to garnish
¾ cup (75g) **bean sprouts**
½ cup (50g) **snap peas,** finely sliced on the diagonal
1 **red chilli,** sliced to garnish (optional)

Put the stock into a large saucepan and bring to a boil. Add the palm sugar, fish sauce and lime juice. Then add the cubes of fish. Bring gently to a boil, then reduce the heat and simmer for about 5 minutes or until the fish is cooked. Turn off the heat and stir in the coriander, bean sprouts and snap peas. Serve immediately with an extra sprig of coriander and a few chilli slices if you like.

◼ *Shrimp are a great alternative to white fish in this soup.*

Pork, chilli and Chinese cabbage soup

Hot-sour-salty-sweet

This soup captures the flavors that characterize Thai cooking.

Serves 6

1lb 2oz (500g) **ground pork, chicken or turkey**
1 **small green chilli,** deseeded and finely chopped
2 Tbsp **soy sauce**
1 Tbsp **sesame oil**
6¼ cups (1.5L) **chicken stock (see page 12)**
1 **head Chinese cabbage,** shredded

For the flavorings:
1 **red onion,** finely chopped
3 Tbsp **finely chopped coriander**
3 Tbsp **finely chopped mint**
1 Tbsp **finely chopped fresh ginger**
1 Tbsp **finely chopped garlic**
1 tsp **red chilli paste** or to taste
¼ cup (50ml) **lime juice**
scant ½ cup (100ml) **lemon juice**
4 Tbsp **fish sauce**
2 Tbsp **palm or brown sugar**

In a large bowl combine the pork, chilli, soy sauce and oil. Heat a
large saucepan over medium-high heat. Add the pork mixture and
cook, breaking up the meat with a spoon. When almost cooked,
add the stock, bring to a boil, then simmer for 5 minutes.

Meanwhile, combine the flavorings and set aside. Two minutes
before serving add the cabbage and simmer until just tender. Add
the flavorings, heat through for just 1 minute and serve
immediately. Note – the greens lose their luster when re-heated.

Mulligatawny

Pepper water

There are as many versions of this spicy, Anglo-Indian soup as there are explanations for its origin. What they all have in common, however, is a meaty stock, warming vegetables and varying degrees of curry-kick. Our version, featuring a lamb shank and a tart green apple, is the best around.

Serves 4–6

2 Tbsp **olive oil**
1 **lamb shank**
  about 1lb (450g)
1 **large onion,**
  finely chopped
2 **carrots,** diced
1 **parsnip,** diced
1 **potato,** diced
¼ cup (50g) **uncooked basmati rice**
2–3 Tbsp **mild curry paste**
6¼ cups (1.5L) **lamb, chicken or vegetable stock (see pages 12–13)**
½ tsp **salt**
¼ tsp **freshly ground black pepper**
1 **Granny Smith apple,** peeled, cored and chopped

Heat oil in a large saucepan over medium-high heat. Brown the lamb shank in the oil, turning, until all sides are golden brown. Add the onion and cook for 3–5 minutes, stirring, until golden. Add the carrots, parsnip, potato, basmati rice and curry paste, stir until fragrant. Add the stock, season with salt and pepper, and bring to a boil. Reduce the heat to medium-low, cover and simmer for 45 minutes.

Remove the lamb shank and cool slightly. Strip the meat away from the shank and return the meat to the pot, discarding the bone. Season, add the apple and stir. Gently re-heat and serve.

▨ *Serve this soup with warm Naan bread (see page 164).*

▨ *Mulligatawny means "pepper water." That said, add curry paste according to taste!*

Mulligatawny

Shrimp laksa

Shrimp laksa

Spicy

Typically Singaporean, the classic Laksa is made with shrimp, but try it with any other seafood or firm fish or chicken.

Serves 4

2 large red chillies, roughly chopped
6 shallots, chopped
3 cloves garlic, roughly chopped
2-in (5-cm) piece fresh ginger, roughly chopped
1 tsp coriander seeds, toasted and finely ground
1 stalk lemongrass, finely sliced
½ cup (10g) coriander leaves
1 tsp ground turmeric
2 Tbsp peanut oil
3½ cups (800ml) coconut milk
1¾ cups (400ml) fish or vegetable stock (see pages 13–14)
2 Tbsp fish sauce
1lb 2oz (500g) raw king shrimp, peeled
7oz (200g) rice vermicelli noodles, cooked
Juice of 1 lime
1½ cups (150g) bean sprouts
3 spring onions, finely sliced

Put the chillies, shallots, garlic, ginger, coriander seeds, lemongrass, coriander leaves and turmeric in a food processor with 1 Tbsp of the peanut oil and purée to a coarse paste.

Heat the remaining 1 Tbsp oil in a stockpot and fry the paste for 1 minute, stirring well. Add the coconut milk and stock and bring to a boil. Reduce the heat and simmer for 10 minutes before adding the fish sauce and shrimp. Stir gently, then add the noodles. Bring back to a boil, turn off the heat, add the lime juice and bean sprouts, then serve immediately. Garnish with a few slices of spring onion.

Romesco soup

Piquant

Romesco is a sauce with origins in the Middle East. It is a favorite of ours, which we knew would be divine as a soup.

Serves 6

¾ cup (100g) **blanched almonds**
½ cup (50g) **shelled hazelnuts**
2 **red peppers**
1 **long red chilli pepper,** about 2in (5cm) in length
8 Tbsp **olive oil**
4 **cloves garlic**
2¼oz (60g) **stale crusty white bread,** about 3–4 slices, **cubed**
24-oz (796-ml) can **stewed tomatoes**
1 Tbsp **tomato purée or paste**
2¼ cups (500ml) **whole milk**
1 tsp **salt**
¼ tsp **black pepper**

Preheat the oven to 350°F/180°C.

Place the nuts on a baking sheet and toast on the top shelf of the oven for 15–20 minutes or until golden. Set aside. Roast the peppers and chilli pepper (see page 19). Place in a bowl and cover with plastic wrap. When cool, peel off the skin and discard the seeds. Set aside.

Heat 4 Tbsp oil in a large frying pan. Gently sauté the garlic cloves until golden. Remove with a slotted spoon and set aside. Add the bread and fry until golden. Remove from the heat.

Combine the peppers, chilli pepper, nuts, garlic, bread, tomatoes, tomato purée and the remaining olive oil in a bowl and stir to combine. Working in batches, purée the mixture until it's as smooth as possible, but don't strain it. Transfer to a large pot and place over medium heat. Add the milk, salt and pepper, and stir. Simmer gently and serve.

Romesco soup

Chorizo, squash and barley soup

Hearty

The spicy chorizo adds a bit of fire to this dish, but, if you prefer, choose a milder chorizo or other sausage instead.

Serves 4

4 Tbsp **olive oil**
1 **onion,** finely chopped
2 **cloves garlic,**
   finely chopped
2 **celery sticks,** finely sliced
1 **red chilli,** deseeded
   and finely chopped
scant 1 cup (200g)
   uncooked pearl barley
4½ cups (1.5L) **cold water**
1lb 10oz (750g) **butternut**
   squash, deseeded and
   chopped into ⅝-in
   (1.5-cm) cubes
½ cup (10g) **sage leaves,**
   finely chopped
12oz (350g) **spicy (picante)**
   chorizo, halved
   lengthwise then sliced
½ cup (10g) **parsley,** finely
   chopped

Preheat the oven to 400°F/200°C. Heat 2 Tbsp of the oil in a large saucepan. Sauté the onion, garlic, celery and chilli for 3–4 minutes, or until the onion is translucent and slightly golden. Add the barley and toss to coat in a layer of oil. Add the water and bring to a boil. Reduce the heat and simmer for 1–1¼ hours or until the barley is tender.

While the barley is cooking put the remaining oil in a roasting pan and toss the squash and sage in it. Roast for 20–25 minutes. Add the chorizo and toss together with the squash. Return to the oven for a further 15 minutes or until golden and the chorizo oils are oozing. Remove from the oven and set aside. When the barley is tender to the bite, stir in the squash, sage and chorizo and bring back to a boil. Stir in the parsley and serve. The barley keeps absorbing liquid. If you do not serve immediately add extra water or stock and bring back to a boil before serving.

Spicy harissa lamb and Puy lentil soup

Wholesome

Harissa is a fragrant chilli paste of North African origin. This soup makes a deliciously hearty and nutritious meal.

Serves 4

1 Tbsp **olive oil**
2 **lamb shanks,** about
  2lb 4oz (1kg)
2 **carrots,** finely diced
2 **celery sticks,**
  finely chopped
1 **onion,** finely diced
3–4 Tbsp **harissa paste,**
  to taste
3½ cups (800ml) **lamb
  stock (see page 19)**
scant 1 cup (200ml) **red
  wine**
14-oz (400-g) can
  chopped tomatoes,
  sieved
3 **bay leaves**
generous 1 cup (250g) **Puy
  lentils**
1 tsp **cornstarch** dissolved
  in 1 Tbsp water **(optional)**
1 cup (20g) **flat-leaf
  parsley,** chopped

Heat the oil in a large stockpot. Add the lamb and cook, turning, until golden all over. Remove the shanks and set aside. Add the carrots, celery and onion and sauté until the onion is translucent. Add the harissa paste and stir. Add the stock, wine, tomatoes and bay leaves to the pan together with the lamb. Bring to a boil, then reduce the heat and simmer, covered, for 1½–2 hours or until the lamb is cooked and starting to fall off the bone. Add the lentils after 1 hour of cooking and continue cooking for the remaining 30 minutes to 1 hour. Turn off the heat and allow to stand for 15 minutes. Remove the shanks from the pot. Discard the bay leaves.

Add the cornstarch and water mixture and stir well. Pull the lamb from the bones and tear into bite-sized pieces. Return the meat to the pan with most of the parsley. Bring back to a boil before serving and garnish with extra parsley and extra harissa if you like.

Chicken dumpling and noodle soup

Chicken dumpling and noodle soup

Fragrant

This aromatic soup is a take on the more traditional chicken noodle soup. I have given it a Vietnamese twist with Oriental chicken dumplings, a note of chilli and fragrant herbs.

Serves 4

4½ cups (1.5L) **Oriental stock (see page 14)**
  or stock made using Tom Yum stock cubes

For the dumplings:
14oz (400g) **skinless, boneless chicken pieces**
¼oz (10g) **fresh ginger,** finely grated
½ cup (10g) **mint leaves**
½ cup (10g) **coriander leaves,** plus extra to garnish
1 tsp **sesame oil**
1 Tbsp **sweet soy sauce**
1 **large red chilli,** halved, deseeded and roughly chopped
1 Tbsp **cornstarch**

5½oz (150g) **thin rice noodles,** broken in half
2 **carrots,** julienned
1½ cups (150g) **bean sprouts**

Put the stock in a large saucepan and bring to a boil. Reduce the heat and simmer while you prepare the dumplings.

Chop the chicken and put in a food processor. Add the ginger, mint, coriander, sesame oil, soy sauce, chilli and cornstarch. Process until well combined. Shape the dumpling mixture into teaspoon-sized balls and drop into the stock. Add the noodles and the carrots to the stock. Simmer for a further 8–10 minutes or until the dumplings and noodles are cooked. Stir in the bean sprouts and extra coriander and serve.

Indian spiced lentil and tomato soup

Aromatic

A fusion of lentils and cardamom, chillies, turmeric, star anise and a hint of coconut cream takes a homely lentil soup to entirely new levels. Serve with pita crisps (see below).

Serves 6

2 large ripe tomatoes
2 Tbsp **vegetable oil**
1 large onion, finely diced
4 **cloves garlic,**
    finely chopped
1 **red chilli,** deseeded
    and finely chopped
1 tsp **ground cardamom**
1 tsp **ground turmeric**
1 **whole star anise**
generous 1 cup (250g) **Puy**
    lentils, rinsed
4½ cups (1L) **vegetable**
    stock (see page 13)
2 Tbsp **fish sauce**
Juice of 1 lemon
2oz (50g) **creamed coconut**
½ tsp **salt**
¼ tsp **black pepper**
Pita bread, to serve
Olive oil, for brushing
Sea salt and black pepper

Skin the tomatoes (see page 19). Chop the tomatoes into quarters, discard the seeds and finely chop. Set aside. Heat the oil in a stockpot over medium heat. Add the tomato, onion, garlic, chilli, cardamom, turmeric and star anise and stir until the onion softens, about 5 minutes. Stir in the lentils and stock and simmer, partially covered, until the lentils are tender, about 25 minutes. Add the fish sauce, lemon juice and coconut cream and stir until the coconut cream has melted. Add salt and pepper.

Preheat oven to 400°F/200°C. Slice the pita bread in half horizontally with a serrated knife. Cut the pita halves into triangles. Place on a baking tray. Brush both sides with olive oil, sprinkle with sea salt and pepper and bake until crisp and golden.

Indian spiced lentil and tomato soup

Special Occasions

Whether it's a holiday, a reunion, a birthday or an anniversary, why not say it with soup? After all, even soup deserves its moment in the sun. It can't always be soothing, medicinal, hearty and warming. Sometimes it just wants to shine, to impress, to sparkle. A special occasion is the perfect opportunity for soup to come into its own.

In order to make an impact, a soup to be served at a special occasion must feature a special ingredient that makes the diner sit up and take notice. It's the luxurious additions, those special touches that elevate soup to an elegant status worthy of a celebration.

Remember, however, that what some regard as luxury may be commonplace fare to others. So don't, for example, serve lobster bisque to a Nova Scotia fisherman. They've been eating lobster since time immemorial.

Emily Post would say a fine soup requires appropriate etiquette. Sit up, elbows off the table, tip the bowl forward, and don't lick the ladle – even when it's dripping with the most delicious soup.

Bouillabaisse

Satisfying

Topped with garlicky rouille and crispy croûtons on the side, this special soup makes a superb dinner-party starter.

Serves 4

2 Tbsp **olive oil**
1 **onion,** finely chopped
1 **leek,** finely sliced
1 **celery stick,** finely sliced
1 **red chilli,** finely chopped
3 **bay leaves**
3 **cloves garlic,** chopped
2 Tbsp **tomato purée or paste**
1 Tbsp **chilli paste** (optional)
generous 1 cup (250ml) **dry white wine**
1 pinch **saffron strands**
1 tsp **extra fine sugar**
14-oz (400-g) can **chopped tomatoes**
3 cups (750ml) **fish stock** (see page 14)
Sea salt and black pepper
1lb 2oz (500g) **firm fish** (e.g. cod) cut into cubes
14oz (400g) **mussels,** preferably green-lipped
8–12 **raw shrimp**

To serve:
2 Tbsp **chopped parsley**
Rouille (see page 161)
Croûtons (see page 156)

Heat the oil in a large saucepan or stockpot. Add the onion and sauté until translucent. Add the leek, celery, chilli, bay leaves and garlic and sauté until soft but not browned, about 3–4 minutes. Stir in the tomato purée and chilli paste, if using, then add the white wine, saffron, sugar, tomatoes and stock. Bring to a boil and season to taste. Reduce to a simmer and add the fish, mussels and shrimp. Simmer for a further 5 minutes, or until the fish is flaky, the mussels have opened (discard any that do not open) and the shrimp have changed color from blue to bright pink.

Ladle into bowls and serve topped with chopped parsley, a spoonful of rouille and croûtons on the side.

Bouillabaisse

Oxtail and butter bean soup

Rich

This soup was inspired by my mother, Janet. You could use lamb shanks instead of oxtail if you prefer.

Serves 4

¼ cup (50g) **flour, for dusting**
Salt and black pepper
2lb 4oz (1kg) **oxtail pieces
  or lamb shanks**
1 Tbsp **olive oil**
1 **onion,** finely chopped
1 **celery stick,** finely diced
1 **clove garlic,** finely
  chopped
3 **bay leaves**
**Finely grated rind of
  2 oranges**
3 **cinnamon sticks**
1 tsp **ground ginger**
1½ tsp **smoked paprika**
5 cups (1.2L) **beef stock
  (see page 13)**
1¼ cups (300ml) **red wine**
1½ cups (250g) **dried butter
  beans,** cooked **(see
  pages 19–20)**
¼ cup (10g) **chopped
  parsley**
**Preserved lemon pieces,
  to garnish**

Season the flour generously with salt and pepper and use to dust the oxtail pieces lightly. Heat the oil in a large stockpot and sauté the oxtail in batches until golden all over. Remove from the pan and set aside, leaving any residue behind.

Add the onion and celery to the pan and sauté until the onion is translucent. Add the garlic and bay leaves, orange rind and spices and sauté for a further minute. Add the stock and red wine and bring to a boil. Reduce to a simmer and put the oxtail pieces back in the pan. Cover and simmer for 2–2½ hours or until the meat is falling off the bone. After 1½ hours add the cooked butter beans to the pan and remove the lid. You can either remove the meat from the bones before serving and discard the bones, or keep the bones in to chew on. Serve topped with chopped parsley and preserved lemon pieces.

Duck soup with orange and Earl Grey

Mysterious

It's duck soup – decadent, deeply, mysteriously flavorful, and, as the expression suggests, really not that difficult.

Serves 6

2 Tbsp **butter (or duck fat drippings)**
7oz (200g) **shallots,** finely sliced
4 **spring onions,** white and pale green parts only, (tops reserved), finely sliced
2 Tbsp **fresh ginger,** grated
9 cups (2L) **duck stock see page 12),** skimmed of fat
1 Tbsp **orange zest**
1½ cups (350ml) **good-quality orange juice,** preferably fresh
6 tsp **Earl Grey tea leaves** or take the leaves out of 6 Earl Grey tea bags
2 **star anise**
4 **cloves**
2 Tbsp **honey**
Duck meat from carcass, shredded
1 tsp **salt**
½ tsp **ground black pepper**

To garnish:
2 **oranges,** peeled and thinly sliced crossways

Reserved spring onion tops, sliced on the diagonal

Heat the butter in a large stockpot over medium heat. Add the shallots, sliced spring onions and ginger and sauté until golden, about 5 minutes. Add 2¼ cups (500ml) stock, orange zest, juice, tea leaves, star anise and cloves. Bring to a boil and simmer until the mixture has reduced almost by half, about 30 minutes.

Pour the liquid through a sieve, pushing with the back of a spoon to extract as much liquid as possible. Return the soup to the pan. Add the remaining stock, honey, duck meat, salt and pepper and simmer for 10 minutes.

Garnish with the oranges and the spring onion tops.

Black cod, soba and bok choy soup

Black cod, soba and bok choy soup

Delicate

Allow at least 24 hours marinating time for the cod. The result is meltingly delicious fish.

Serves 6

For the cod:
1lb (450g) **cod fillet, skinned**
6 Tbsp (75ml) **rice wine**
6 Tbsp (75ml) **mirin**
1 Tbsp (75g) **miso paste**
1 Tbsp **soy sauce**
1 Tbsp **brown sugar**

For the dashi:
4-in (10-cm) **square piece dried kelp**
6¼ cups (1.5L) **cold water**
1 tsp **bonito flakes**

For the soup:
9oz (250g) **soba noodles**
⅔ cup (150ml) **mirin**
4 Tbsp **soy sauce**
6 **heads bok choy,** cut in half lengthwise
Sesame seeds, to garnish

Chop the cod into 1½-in (4-cm) pieces. Combine the rice wine, mirin, miso paste, soy sauce and brown sugar in a large, shallow bowl. Add the cod, toss to coat, cover with plastic wrap and refrigerate for 24–48 hours.

Before serving, cook the noodles according to the instructions. Drain and divide between six bowls.

Soak the dried kelp in the water in a large saucepan until it doubles in size. Bring to a boil, immediately remove the kelp and discard. Add the bonito flakes and boil for 10 seconds. Remove from the heat and allow to stand for 1 minute, then strain through a fine sieve lined with muslin. Return the dashi to the pot. Add the mirin and soy sauce and simmer over medium heat. Remove the cod from the marinade with a slotted spoon and add to the pan, together with the bok choy. Simmer for 4 minutes. Spoon the cod and bok choy over the noodles, then pour over the dashi. Garnish.

Clam, saffron and orzo soup

Delectable

It is always best to serve this soup immediately if you can. Orzo is a small pasta shape so it will keep absorbing the liquid the longer it sits.

Serves 4

2 Tbsp **olive oil**
4 **shallots,** finely chopped
1 **red chilli,** deseeded and finely chopped
3 **cloves garlic,** bruised
3 **bay leaves**
1lb 2oz (500g) **clams**
scant 1 cup (200ml) **white wine**
4½ cups (1L) **fish stock (see page 14)**
1 **pinch saffron threads**
1 cup (250g) **orzo**
3 Tbsp **chopped fresh herbs of choice (parsley, coriander, tarragon, oregano, chives)**
Juice of 1 **lemon**
¼ cup (50ml) **heavy cream** (optional)
Sea salt and freshly ground black pepper

Heat the olive oil in a large saucepan or stockpot. Add the shallots and chilli and sauté until the shallots are translucent, about 5 minutes. Add the garlic and bay leaves and sauté for a further minute. Add the clams and wine, cover and shake to steam the clams open. As they open, remove them from the pan until all are removed and set aside. Discard any clams that do not open.

Add the stock and saffron to the pan and bring to a boil, then add the orzo. Reduce the heat and simmer for about 5 minutes or until the orzo is cooked.

Return the clams to the pan with the chopped herbs and lemon juice. Stir to combine. Add the heavy cream, if you wish, and season with salt and pepper to taste. Serve immediately.

Clam, saffron and orzo soup

Jerusalem artichoke soup

Jerusalem artichoke soup

Perfection

Jerusalem artichokes are one of those heavenly vegetables I simply can't live without. It wasn't until I came to London that I tasted them for the first time, and there's been no going back since then. For such a simple soup, this is delicious and made a little bit more indulgent with a drizzle of truffle oil.

Serves 4

1 Tbsp **olive oil**
1 **onion,** finely chopped
2 **celery sticks,** sliced
1 **clove garlic,** crushed
1lb 7oz (650g) **Jerusalem artichokes,** peeled and chopped into chunks
5 cups (1.2L) **chicken stock (see page 12)**
⅔ cup (150ml) **heavy cream**

To serve:
Jerusalem artichoke shavings (see page 160)
Truffle oil (optional)

Heat the oil in a large saucepan or stockpot. Add the onion and celery and sauté until the onion is translucent. Add the garlic and Jerusalem artichoke chunks and sauté for a further 2 minutes, stirring frequently. Add the stock and bring to a boil. Reduce the heat and simmer uncovered for 15–20 minutes or until the artichokes are tender and starting to break apart. Turn off the heat and allow to stand for 5 minutes.

Transfer the soup to a blender, in two batches, and purée to a smooth consistency. Return to the pan, add the cream and bring to a boil before serving. Ladle into bowls and garnish with artichoke shavings and a drizzle of truffle oil if liked.

■ *If you don't have any truffle oil, then a drizzle of your finest extra virgin olive oil will be delicious as well.*

Lobster bisque

Decadent

This recipe was given to me by friend, recipe tester and inspired cook Cynthia Shupe.

Serves 4–6

For the stock:
2 **cooked lobsters,** each
   1lb 9oz (700g), rinsed
   under cold running water
½ cup (100ml) **white wine**
1 **bay leaf**
10 **peppercorns**
1 **onion,** peeled and halved
1 **pinch salt**
6¼ cups (1.5L) **water**

For the soup:
4 Tbsp **butter**
2 Tbsp **olive oil**
¾ cup (100g) **finely
   chopped onion**
½ cup (100g) **finely
   chopped celery**
4 Tbsp **flour**
2¼ cups (500ml)
   half-and-half
generous 1 cup (250ml)
   tomato juice
2¼ cups (500ml) **lobster
   stock (see above)**
Salt and pepper to taste

Crack lobster shells (reserve), pick out the meat and cut into small pieces. Set aside. To make the lobster stock place the shells in a large, heavy-based saucepan and add the remaining stock ingredients. Cover with water and bring to a boil. Simmer, partly covered, for 45 minutes, occasionally skimming impurities. Strain and reserve.

Melt the butter and olive oil in a heavy-based saucepan over low heat. Add the onion, cover and cook for 5 minutes until soft. Add the celery and sauté for a further 5 minutes. Add the flour, stirring continuously for 2 minutes until smooth. Add the half-and-half and stir until slightly thickened, about 5 minutes. Add the tomato juice, 2¼ cups (500ml) of the reserved stock (freeze any remaining stock for future use) and the salt and pepper. Before serving, stir through the cooked lobster pieces, being careful not to allow the soup to boil.

Lobster bisque

Mushroom and chestnut soup

Meaty

This soup is rich and almost meaty in texture. It makes an elegant starter if you are entertaining vegetarian guests. It is served with arugula cream (instructions below!).

Serves 4

¼ cup (20g) **dried porcini mushrooms**
1lb 5oz (600g) **mixed fresh wild mushrooms,** washed and dried
2 Tbsp **olive oil**
2 **cloves garlic,** finely chopped
1lb 2-oz (500-g) bottle or can **tomato passata**
1¾ cups (400ml) **chicken stock (see page 12)**
9-oz (240-g) can **whole peeled and cooked chestnuts
(vacuum-packed)**
Salt and freshly ground black pepper
1 cup (50g) **fresh arugula leaves,** plus extra leaves to garnish
½ cup (100ml) **heavy cream**

Soak the dried porcini in boiling water for at least 15 minutes. While the porcini are soaking, chop the fresh wild mushrooms into thin slices.

Heat the oil in a large saucepan. Add the garlic and sauté until just golden, then add the fresh mushrooms. Drain the porcini, reserving ½ cup (100ml) of the soaking liquid, and finely chop. Add the chopped porcini to the pan and continue stirring. Add the tomato passata, chicken stock, reserved porcini soaking liquid and chestnuts and season to taste. Bring to a boil, reduce the heat and simmer, uncovered, for 15–20 minutes.

Meanwhile, put the arugula and cream in a blender and liquidize until smooth. Serve the soup with a drizzle of arugula cream and extra arugula leaves for garnish.

Oyster soup with crispy leeks

Exuberant

The late Mme. Benoit was a cookbook writer from Quebec who celebrated local, seasonal Canadian cooking long before it was à la mode. This recipe, based on Mme. Benoit's, is a rich, glorious way to celebrate the luxury of oysters.

Serves 4

2¼ cups (500ml) **shucked oysters and their juice** (if short on liquid, supplement with clam juice to make up 2¼ cups (500ml)
1¼ sticks (150g) **butter**
2 Tbsp **olive oil**
1 **medium onion,** finely chopped
2 **celery sticks,** finely chopped
2 **carrots,** grated
1 **leek,** white and pale green part only, finely chopped
1¼ cups (150g) **flour**
6 Tbsp (75ml) **half-and-half**
½ cup (125ml) **sherry or Madeira**
Salt and pepper to taste
Crispy leeks (see page 153)

Pick over the oysters to ensure they are free from any bits of shell. Drain the oysters and reserve the liquid.

Melt the butter with the olive oil in a heavy-based saucepan over low heat. Add the onion, cover and cook for 5 minutes until soft. Add the celery, carrot and leek, stirring well to combine. Add the flour, stirring continuously for 2 minutes to get rid of any lumps. Add the half-and-half and oyster liquid and stir until thickened.

Before serving, add the sherry or Madeira and stir well. Then add the oysters and cook gently over low heat until the oysters become plump and curl around the edges. Season with salt and pepper and top with the crispy leeks.

Tomato soup with dumplings

Mediterranean

China meets Greece meets Italy in this sophisticated, intensively flavored soup with feta cheese and spinach dumplings. Look for wonton wrappers, either fresh or frozen, in Oriental grocery stores or specialty food shops.

Serves 4–6

For the soup:
Tomato soup
  (see page 47)

For the feta and spinach
  dumplings:
1 Tbsp **olive oil**
5 **spring onions,** white
  and pale parts only,
  finely chopped
9oz (250g) **fresh spinach**
½ cup (100g) cubed **feta
  cheese**
½ cup (100g) **ricotta cheese**
1 Tbsp **chopped fresh dill**
¼ tsp **black pepper**
Flour for sprinkling
24 **wonton wrappers**

Heat the oil in a large frying pan over medium heat. Add the spring onions and sauté for 2–3 minutes. Add the spinach and stir until wilted. Transfer to a bowl and add the feta, ricotta, dill and black pepper. Stir to combine.

Line a baking tray with parchment paper and sprinkle with a little flour. Place the wonton wrappers on the parchment and spoon 1 tsp of the filling into the center of each wrapper. Run a wet finger around the edge of the skin, one square at a time. Fold in half to form a triangle and seal the edges.

Pour 9 cups (2L) water into a large saucepan and bring to a gentle boil. Add the dumplings and cook until they float to the surface, about 2 minutes. Remove with a slotted spoon and divide among the bowls of hot tomato soup.

Tomato soup with dumplings

Wild rice and porcini soup

Wild rice and porcini soup

Robust

The name is deceptive. Wild rice is actually a long marsh grass that is native to the American Great Lakes area.

Serves 4

5½oz (150g) **wild rice, rinsed**
1 **bay leaf**
1¼pt (750ml) **beef stock**
  (see page 13)
2 Tbsp **butter**
12oz (350g) **button**
  mushrooms, sliced
¼ cup (20g) **dried porcini**
  mushrooms, cover with
  1¼ cups (300ml) boiling
  water, soak for 30
  minutes, strain and
  reserve liquid, chopped
1 Tbsp **olive oil**
1 **large onion,** chopped
2 **cloves garlic,** chopped
1 Tbsp **finely chopped**
  rosemary, plus sprigs to
  garnish
1 **potato,** chopped
1 tsp **salt**
½ tsp **black pepper**
generous 1 cup (250ml)
  half-and-half
2 Tbsp **Madeira**

Place rice in a saucepan with the bay leaf and 1 cup (250m) stock. Cover and bring to boil. Stir once, cover, reduce the heat to low and simmer for 40 minutes.

Heat 1 Tbsp of butter in a large saucepan over medium heat. Sauté the button and porcini mushrooms until the button mushrooms are golden. Set aside.

Heat the remaining butter and oil in the same pot and sauté the onion over medium-low heat until translucent, about 10 minutes. Add the garlic, rosemary and potato and sauté until fragrant, 2–3 minutes. Add the remaining stock and dried mushroom soaking liquid and simmer until potatoes are tender. Purée the soup until smooth and return to the pan. Add the salt, pepper, cream and Madeira and stir to combine over low heat. Add the mushrooms and rice. Thin with more stock if necessary.

Accompaniments

Coconut sambal

Makes approx. 1 cup (250g)

2 **cloves garlic,** crushed
1 cup (20g) **coriander leaves**
¾ cup (100g) **roasted peanuts,** unsalted
Grated rind and juice of 1 **lime**
1 **red chilli,** deseeded and finely chopped
Peanut oil if needed
1½ cups (100g) **desiccated coconut**

Put all the ingredients except the coconut in a food processor and blend to a paste, adding 1 Tbsp peanut oil if necessary to obtain the right consistency. Stop blending and stir in the desiccated coconut to combine. Store in an airtight container in the fridge for up to 2 weeks.

Crispy shallots

3 Tbsp **vegetable oil**
6 **shallots,** finely sliced
1 tsp **cumin seeds**
1 tsp **mustard seeds**
1 tsp **sesame seeds**
1 Tbsp **finely chopped parsley**
½ tsp **smoked paprika**

In a small non-stick frying pan heat the vegetable oil until hot. Add the shallots and seeds and sauté, stirring occasionally until golden brown and crispy. Turn off the heat, stir in the chopped parsley and paprika, then transfer to a piece of paper towel to drain off any excess oil.

Cheese straws

I like to add a little pinch of chilli powder or paprika to these cheese straws for an extra bit of fieriness. They are delicious served with Roasted pumpkin soup (see page 44).

Makes approx. 24–36 (depending on length)

1lb 2-oz (500-g) package puff pastry
¾ cup (100g) mixed grated Parmesan and Gruyère cheese

Preheat the oven to 400°F/200°C. Roll out the pastry on a lightly floured board and sprinkle with the cheese mixture. Fold the pastry over three times and roll out again to about ¼in (5mm) thick. Cut the rolled pastry into ½-in (1-cm) wide strips and twist them, holding both ends. Put on a baking sheet and bake for 10–15 minutes, or until golden brown and puffy.

Crispy leeks

2 leeks, white and pale green parts only, trimmed
2¼ cups (500ml) vegetable oil

Cut leeks in half lengthways, then into 1½-in (4-cm) lengths widthways. Then cut lengthwise into very thin julienne strips.

Heat oil in a large, heavy saucepan until it reaches 350°F/180°C. Sauté the leek strips in several batches until golden brown, about 10 seconds. Lift out with a slotted spoon and drain on paper towels. Leave to cool.

■ The crispy leeks can be made up to one day ahead and stored in an airtight container.

Grissini

Makes approx. 36

¼-oz (7-g) **package dried yeast or** ½oz (15g) **fresh yeast**
½ cup (350ml) **lukewarm water**
4½ cups (500g) **white bread flour,** sifted
1 tsp **salt**
2 Tbsp **olive oil**
2 tsp **fine semolina**

To flavor:
Choice of sea salt, sesame seeds, poppy seeds, rosemary, black pepper

Preheat the oven 400°F/200°C.

Sprinkle the yeast into ½ cup (100ml) of the lukewarm water in a small bowl. Leave for 5–10 minutes, then stir to dissolve.

Mix the flour and salt in a large bowl and make a well in the center. Pour in the olive oil and yeasted water. Using a wooden spoon, draw the flour in from the sides, adding the remaining water as needed to form a firm but sticky dough. Turn the dough out onto a lightly floured work surface and knead until it is smooth and elastic, about 10 minutes. Cover the dough with a tea towel and allow to rest for about 10 minutes.

Knead the dough for another 10 minutes. Tear a small amount of dough from the ball at a time and, using the ball of your hand, roll into a long skinny, finger-like shape, about 10in (25cm) long. You can experiment with other shapes and sizes if you like; just adjust the cooking time accordingly.

Lightly oil a baking pan and sprinkle over the semolina. Put the shaped grissini on the tray and flavor with your chosen toppings. Bake in the oven for 15–20 minutes or until golden and crispy. Transfer to a cooling rack and allow to cool.

Grissini

Croûtons

Makes about 24–36

1 Tbsp **olive oil**
2 **cloves garlic, crushed**
1 **baguette, cut into** ½-in (1-cm) diagonal slices

Preheat the oven to 375°F/180°C.

Combine the oil and garlic in a bowl and brush the mixture, using a pastry brush, over both sides of the bread slices. Place on a baking pan and bake for about 15–20 minutes or until crispy and golden.

These will keep in an airtight container for up to 3 weeks.

Rarebit

Makes 4

2 Tbsp **butter**
2 Tbsp **flour**
1 tsp **Dijon mustard**
1 tsp **Worcestershire sauce**
½ tsp **salt**
½ tsp **black pepper**
½ cup (125ml) **beer**
1¼ cups (300ml) **half-and-half**
1½ cups (150g) grated **Cheddar cheese**
2 drops **Tabasco sauce**
4 **slices crusty bread,** toasted

Preheat broiler.

Heat butter and flour in a saucepan over a medium heat, stirring constantly until mixture is golden. Whisk in mustard, Worcestershire sauce, salt and pepper. Whisk until smooth. Whisk in beer and cream and stir until smooth. Add cheese and cook over a low heat for 4–5 minutes, stirring. Add Tobasco sauce and stir.

Place toasted bread slices on a baking pan and pour the cheesy mixture over the bread slices. Place under broiler and cook until golden.

Orange gremolata

Makes 6 Tbsp (enough to garnish 4 bowls)

2 Tbsp **finely chopped flat-leaf parsley**
2 Tbsp **finely chopped fennel fronds**
4 tsp **chopped garlic**
2 tsp **grated orange rind**
1 Tbsp **olive oil**
½ tsp **sea salt**

Place all the ingredients in a bowl and stir to combine.

Dill pesto

Makes ½ cup (125ml)

½ cup (50g) crumbled **feta cheese**
3 Tbsp **pine nuts,** toasted and chopped
1 cup (20g) **dill,** finely chopped
4 Tbsp **olive oil**
Salt and freshly ground black pepper to taste

Combine feta, pine nuts and dill in a bowl and stir to combine. Slowly add the olive oil until the mixture is wet. Add salt and pepper to taste. This hand-chopped pesto, unlike most puréed pestos, is meant to be textured and chunky.

Parsley pesto

Makes 1 cup (250ml)

1 **clove garlic**, roughly chopped
1 **large bunch flat-leaf parsley**, about 2¼–3oz (60–80g)
½ cup (50g) **pine nuts**
½ cup (50g) finely grated **Parmesan cheese**
Grated rind and juice of 1 **lemon**
⅔–scant 1 cup (150–200ml) **olive oil**
Salt and freshly ground black pepper to taste

Put the garlic, parsley, pine nuts, Parmesan, lemon rind and juice in a food processor and process to combine. While the motor is running, drizzle in the olive oil through the feed tube until the desired consistency is reached. Season to taste.

Basil pesto

Makes 1 cup (250ml)

1 large bunch basil, about 60–80g (2¼–3oz)
1 clove garlic, chopped
½ cup (50g) grated Parmesan cheese
½ cup (50g) pine nuts
⅔–¾ cup (150–175ml) extra virgin olive oil
Salt and freshly ground black pepper to taste

Put the basil leaves, garlic, Parmesan, pine nuts and a good splash of the olive oil in a food processor and process until blended. While the motor is still running, slowly add the remaining olive oil through the feed tube until the desired consistency is reached. Season to taste.

Walnut pesto

Makes 1 cup (250ml)

2 cloves garlic, roughly chopped
½ cup (50g) grated Parmesan cheese
¾ cup (100g) fresh shelled walnuts
⅔–1 cup (150–200ml) extra virgin olive oil
¾oz (20g) bunch basil
Salt and freshly ground black pepper to taste

Put the garlic, Parmesan, walnuts and a good splash of olive oil in a food processor and process to a paste. With the motor still running drizzle in the remaining olive oil through the feed tube until the desired consistency is reached. Tear up the basil leaves into the food processor and pulse once or twice to combine, but do not whizz to purée the basil completely. Season to taste.

These tips apply to all of the pesto recipes:
◼ *Parmesan varies in saltiness, so it is important to taste the pesto before seasoning.*

◼ *To store, transfer to a jar or airtight container and cover with a thin layer of oil. Seal and refrigerate for up to 2 weeks.*

Pumpkin seed and parmesan wafers

Makes approx. 24–30

If you are making these for a special occasion, try cooling them over the handle of a wooden spoon to get a tuile shape.

scant 1 cup (50g) **pumpkin seeds or mixture of other seeds**
    e.g. sunflower, sesame, poppy
1 cup (100g) grated **Parmesan cheese**
1 pinch **cayenne**

Preheat the oven to 400°F/200°C and line a baking pan with parchment paper. Combine the pumpkin seeds, Parmesan and cayenne and mix well. Place teaspoonfuls of the mixture on the baking pan, at least 2 in (5cm) apart. Press with the back of a teaspoon so the mixture is evenly spread. Bake in the oven for 10–15 minutes or until crisp and lightly golden. Cool for about 1 minute before transferring to a rack to cool completely.

Root vegetable shavings

1lb 2oz (500g) **root vegetables of choice**
    (parsnip, celeriac, carrot, red beets, sweet potato)
½ cup (100ml) **peanut oil**
Salt

Peel the vegetables and slice them, as thinly as possible, into long strips or rounds using a very sharp knife or mandoline cutter. Heat the oil in a large frying pan until very hot, almost smoking, then fry the vegetables in batches for about 2–3 minutes each. As they cook they will curl up and brown.

When cooked remove with a slotted spoon and drain on paper towels. Make these in advance and store in an airtight container until needed.

Rouille

Makes 1 scant cup (200ml)

1 large potato, boiled
4 cloves garlic, chopped
1 red chilli, chopped
1 egg yolk (see note page 4)
½ tsp paprika
½ cup (100ml) extra virgin olive oil

Place all the ingredients except the oil in a food processor and blend to combine. With the motor still running, pour in the olive oil through the feed tube and continue to blend until well puréed together. The rouille will keep in the fridge for up to 3 days in an airtight container or jar.

Tomato jalapeño salsa

Makes 1 cup (250ml)

¾ cup (250g) cherry tomatoes, cut into quarters
1 fresh jalapeño chilli, finely chopped
½ cup (50g) finely chopped red onion
Juice of 1 lemon
¾ cup (15g) finely chopped coriander
¼ tsp sea salt
Black pepper to taste

Toss all the ingredients together in a small bowl and spoon over hot soup.

Tzatziki

This Greek dip makes a perfect addition to many soups. Try a dollop on Moroccan spiced carrot soup (see page 88) or Avocado and cucumber soup (see page 98).

Makes approx. 10fl oz (300ml)

½ cucumber, halved, seeded and finely diced
1 tsp fine salt
generous 1 cup (250ml) Greek yogurt
2 cloves garlic, crushed
1 Tbsp chopped mint
1 Tbsp chopped dill
2 Tbsp extra virgin olive oil
Grated rind and juice of 1 lemon
Salt and freshly ground black pepper to taste

Put the diced cucumber in a colander or sieve and sprinkle over the fine salt. Stir to combine and leave the cucumber to release its juices for about 10 minutes.

Rinse the cucumber under cold running water and drain on paper towels. Mix the cucumber with all the remaining ingredients and season to taste. Chill well before serving.

Herb and flower ice cubes

Makes 12

12 herb leaves (mint, basil, coriander, or edible flowers)
Water

In a 12-cube ice cube tray, fill each compartment three-quarters full with water and freeze until solid. Remove from the freezer and place a leaf or flower on each cube so it lies flat. Top with water and return to the freezer until frozen solid. Remove from the freezer just prior to using.

Wonton croûtons

Wonton wrappers keep well in the freezer so this is the perfect emergency recipe. Just defrost, and they can be ready in minutes.

Makes 75

Peanut oil for frying
1 **packet small wonton wrappers** (about 75)
Sea salt

Choice of toppings:
1 cup (100g) **sesame seeds,** black or white or a mixture of both
1 cup (100g) **poppy seeds**
1 Tbsp **paprika mixed with** 1 Tbsp **sea salt**

Fill a large wok or saucepan one-third full with peanut oil. Heat the oil to 375°F/190°C, or until a small cube of bread browns in about 30 seconds. Lay the wonton wrappers, six at a time, on a chopping board or flat surface. Using a pastry brush, brush each wrapper with a little water and sprinkle over a little of your choice of topping. Add the wonton wrappers to the hot oil and fry for about 25–30 seconds or until golden brown and crispy. Remove from the oil, drain on paper towels and sprinkle with salt. Once cooled, these can be stored in an airtight container for up to 1 week.

Wonton wrappers come in various sizes, from large, about 4in (10cm), to small, about 2¾in (7cm). If you like, you can cut the wrappers down to smaller sizes for bite-sized croûtons.

Naan bread

Naan bread is a leavened flatbread that originated in the Punjab region of India. These are best eaten while still hot and fresh and are a delicious accompaniment to many of our chicken-based or spicy soups.

Makes 12–16

3 cups (350g) **flour**
1 tsp **fine salt**
1½ tsp **extra-fine sugar**
½ tsp **baking powder**
⅔ cup (150ml) **warm milk**
⅔ cup (150ml) **plain unsweetened yogurt**
¼-oz (7-g) **package dried yeast or** ½oz (15g) **fresh yeast**
2 Tbsp **sunflower oil**
¼ cup (50g) **melted butter**
3 Tbsp **black mustard seeds**

Mix the flour, salt, sugar and baking powder together in a large bowl with a wooden spoon and make a well in the center. Combine the warm milk, yogurt and yeast and add to the well. Stir gently to combine, drawing the flour into the wet mixture. When the mixture is combined, transfer it to a floured surface and knead for about 10 minutes or until smooth, stiff and elastic. Put the dough in a clean bowl and cover with a tea towel. Leave to rise until doubled in size, about 3–4 hours.

Punch the mixture down and divide into 12–16 portions on a floured board. Shape each portion into a teardrop shape and set aside.

Preheat a baking sheet under the broiler for about 2 minutes. Heat the sunflower oil in a large non-stick frying pan. Add the shaped naans, in batches, cooking only one side until the bases are golden and the naans start to puff up. Brush the top side with melted butter and sprinkle over some mustard seeds. Transfer the naans to the preheated baking pan and broil the uncooked side until golden and puffy, about 2–3 minutes. Repeat until all the naans are made.

As you make the naans, stack them on top of each other and place a damp tea towel over them to prevent them drying out.

Naan bread

Glossary

Adobo sauce
A Mexican, dark red sauce made from ground chillies, herbs and vinegar. Delicious as a marinade or served as a sauce. Chipotle chillies are often packed in Adobo sauce.

Arborio rice
An Italian rice traditionally used for risotto. Each granule is shorter and fatter than other short-grain rices. Its high starch content makes for very smooth, creamy risottos.

Bisque
A soup traditionally made with puréed seafood and thickened with cream. Today, bisques are made with a variety of puréed ingredients, from fowl or tomatoes to wild mushrooms.

Bok choy
A Chinese cabbage that resembles a short bunch of celery with wide, leafy tops.

Bonito flakes
Bonito is a type of tuna, a very popular fish in Japanese cuisine. The dark, oily meat is rarely eaten fresh; it's dried into cubes, which are then ground or shaved before use. These shavings, or flakes, form the base for many Japanese sauces and stocks. The flakes, also known as *katsuobushi*, have a strong, salty flavor and are tan in color.

Bouquet garni
A bouquet garni usually consists of a bay leaf, parsley and thyme sprigs, tied together with a piece of string. It is often used in soups, stews and stocks that require lengthy periods of cooking and is removed at the end of cooking.

Cavalo nero
A very dark-leaved cabbage, similar to kale, originating from Italy.

Chèvre
Goat's cheese.

Chinese rice wine
A sweet, pale, low-alcohol wine made from fermented glutinous rice.

Chipotle chillies
Thick-fleshed jalapeño chillies that have been smoked and dried. The result is a rich, well-flavored, moderately hot chilli.

Chorizo
A pork sausage from Spain and Portugal. It is spiced with paprika and can vary in strength from sweet to mild to spicy (picante), depending on the paprika used. It is available fresh or cured. The fresh variety is what is called for in our soups.

Chowder
A name generally used to describe any creamy, rich, chunky soup. The name comes from the French *chaudière*, the cauldron used by French fishermen when making their seafood stews. Most chowders are made with either cream or milk, with the exception of Manhattan-style chowders, which are made with tomatoes. The ingredients vary from seafood to fish, corn to potatoes.

Coconut milk
Like coconut cream, coconut milk is made by combining water and shredded coconut, simmering, then straining through muslin. The ratio, however, is equal parts water to coconut.

Coriander
Also known as cilantro or Chinese parsley, coriander is a fragrant, parsley-like plant popular in Thai, Indian and Latin American cooking. It is one of the only plants used as both a herb and a spice.

Coriander seeds
Quite different in taste from coriander leaves, coriander is a mild, golden brown, dry-roasted seed used in soups, stews, curry powders, pickling brines and marinades.

Creamed coconut
Made by combining 1 part water to 4 parts shredded coconut, simmered, then strained. It is sold as a thick block wrapped in plastic and packaged in a cardboard box, much like chocolate.

Crème fraîche
A thickened cream – thicker than sour cream – with a tangy, nutty flavor. It can be made by combining 9fl oz (250ml) heavy cream with

2 Tbsp buttermilk. Cover and allow to stand for 8 to 24 hours until very thick. Stir well, then refrigerate for up to 10 days. Crème fraîche is useful in cooking because it won't curdle if boiled and makes an ideal topping for soups.

Curry leaves
Small, delicately spicy green leaves commonly used in Thai and Indian cookery. Curry leaves are found in Indian and Asian grocers. Store fresh leaves in an airtight bag in the freezer, or in the fridge for up to a week. Don't bother buying dried leaves; they have very little flavor.

Farro
A little, light brown cereal grain that's been a mainstay in Tuscan cookery for centuries. Delicious in soups, salads and desserts, farro can be substituted, or vice versa, for pasta, rice and lentils.

Fish sauce
A Southeast Asian condiment made from salted, fermented fish used to salt dishes. The Thai version is called *nam pla*, while the Vietnamese call it *nuoc nam*.

Green-lipped mussels
So-called because of the distinctive green lip around the inside of the shell. They are the largest variety of mussel and are unique to the coastal waters of New Zealand.

Ham hock
The lower portion of a hog's hind leg used to flavor dishes that require low, slow cooking. Most hocks are cured or smoked.

Harissa
A paste of North African origin made of chilli, garlic and spices. It adds a fiery and fragrant note to any dish. Available to buy in gourmet stores.

Jalapeño
A bright green, medium-hot chilli with thick, crisp flesh.

Kelp
The general name for any edible seaweed.

Lamb shank
These are small joints cut from the end of the leg and are also known as knuckle joints. They are very reasonable in price and full of flavor.

Lime leaves

Sometimes sold fresh, but most often frozen, these dark green leaves have an unmistakable Thai-like, citronella flavor. Leaves will keep in an airtight bag in the freezer for several months.

Madeira

A fortified wine named after the Portuguese-owned island off the northwest coast of Africa from which it derives its name. It ranges dramatically in sweetness and color. Madeira is an excellent cooking wine that adds delicious depth to many soups. Although costly, a little goes a long way.

Marsala

A fortified wine from Sicily with an alcohol content of around 20 percent. It is made by mixing grape juice with white wine that is then left to mature. Marsala is often used in cooking, giving a flavor that ranges from sweet to dry.

Mirin

Like Chinese rice wine, mirin is a Japanese low-alcohol, sweet golden wine made from glutinous rice. It adds a distinctive sweetness to soups.

Miso paste

Miso, or bean paste, is a staple in Japanese cooking. It is fermented soybean paste that looks much like peanut butter. There are three categories of miso paste available: barley miso, rice miso and soybean miso. All are injected with a mold, then aged from 6 months to 3 years. Flavor depends on the amount of mold injected, the amount of salt used, and the period of fermentation.

Nori flakes

Made from seaweed. Seaweed includes any edible plant belonging to the algae family. All seaweed is rich in iodine, protein and in vitamins A, B and C. Seaweed is widely used in Asian cooking. Nori sheets are paper-thin seaweed sheets that are mainly used for sushi. The sheets are also sold shredded into nori flakes for use in soups and as a delicious seasoning to rice dishes.

Orzo

A rice-shaped pasta that is often used in soups. It is similar, just slightly larger, than risi.

Palm sugar

This dark, coarse, unrefined sugar, also known as jaggery, can be made either from the sap of palm trees or from sugar-cane juice. It is primarily used in Southeast Asia and comes in several forms – the two most popular being a soft, honey-butter texture and a solid cake-like form.

Pancetta

Italian bacon that has been cured with herbs and spices, rolled and then pressed between boards that flatten it into a block. It can be smoked or unsmoked. It is usually bought in a piece and chopped into cubes or very thin slices before using.

Parmesan cheese

A dry, hard cow's milk cheese with a sharp flavor. Parmesan cheeses are made throughout the world, but the best is Italy's *Parmigiano Reggiano*. It has a grainy, melt-in-the-mouth quality that is due to at least 2 years' aging. Look for the words *Parmigiano Reggiano* on the rind, which means the cheese was produced in and around Parma, where the cheese originated.

Pernod

French alcoholic beverage with a distinctive aniseed flavor.

Preserved lemons

Lemons that have been soaked in salt and lemon juice and left to mature for at least a month before use. The whole fruit is eaten, including the skin and pith. Used in Middle Eastern and North African cooking. Available in bottles or jars.

Puy lentils

Lentils are easy to cook because they don't require presoaking before cooking. There are many varieties, but we like French Puy lentils best for their flavor and good-temperedness. They are tiny, slate-grey-green in color, and retain their shape and texture when cooked.

Rice vermicelli

Fine Chinese noodles made from rice flour.

Sea salt

The salt produced after the evaporation of sea water. It is sold as fine grains or large, flaky crystals. Our favorite is Maldon Sea Salt from the east coast of England. Sprinkled with a few twists of black pepper, it adds flavor and texture to any soup.

Soba
Soba are Japanese noodles made from buckwheat and wheat flour.

Tamarind
The fruit of a shade tree native to Asia. The large pods contain a sweet-sour pulp that is especially sour when dried. Tamarind is used to season many East Indian, Oriental and Middle Eastern dishes in the way lemon juice is used. Sold as a juice, paste or dried and ground into a powder.

Tomato passata
Puréed, sieved tomatoes available in supermarkets in cans, cartons or bottles. It is commonly used in pasta sauces, pizza toppings, and in casseroles and soups.

Udon
Thick Japanese wheat noodles.

Wasabi
The essential condiment for Japanese sushi. Wasabi is made from a horseradish-like plant and adds a fiery and aromatic note to dishes. It is available as a paste or in powder form.

Wild rice
Wild rice, despite its name, isn't rice at all. It is a long, marsh grass native to the Great Lakes area of North America. It is now being harvested in the Canadian prairies, the American Midwest and parts of California. It has a wonderful nutty flavor and chewy texture that adds sophistication to any dish. Wild rice needs a good soaking before cooking, and it often takes 45 minutes – 1 hour to cook.

Wonton wrappers
Also known as wonton skins, they come in various sizes but are usually square. They can be easily trimmed to size using scissors. Wonton wrappers are used in a number of ways, from deep-fried dumplings to steamed spring rolls.

About the authors

Pippa Cuthbert is a New Zealander living and working in London. Ever since childhood she has been passionate about food and cooking. After studying Nutrition and Food Science at Otago University in New Zealand and working in the test kitchen of Nestlé New Zealand, she decided to travel the world in search of new and exciting culinary adventures. Now based in London, Pippa works as a food writer and stylist on books and magazines, and is also involved in advertising and commercials.

Food and writing are **Lindsay Cameron Wilson's** passions, so she blended the two in college where she studied History, Journalism, and the Culinary Arts. She has since worked in the test kitchens of *Canadian Living Magazine* in Toronto and *Sunset Magazine* in San Francisco. In 2001 she left her job as a food columnist in Halifax, Nova Scotia, and moved to London. That's when she met Pippa, and the work for their first book, *JUICE!* began. Fuelled by juice, the two moved on to *Ice Cream!* and now *Soup!* Lindsay continues to work as a food journalist in Canada, where she now lives with her husband, James, and baby, Luke.

Index